Learn to Paint
BIRDS
IN WATERCOLOUR
Peter Partington

COLLINS

First published in 1989
by William Collins Sons & Co., Ltd
London · Glasgow · Sydney
Auckland · Toronto · Johannesburg

© Peter Partington, 1989

Layout by Tim Higgins
Filmset by Ace Filmsetting, Frome, Somerset
Colour reproduction by Bright Arts, Hong Kong
Photography by Nigel Cheffers-Heard

British Library Cataloguing in Publication Data
Partington, Peter
 Learn to paint birds.—(Learn to
 paint series)
 1. Watercolour paintings. Special subjects
 Birds. Techniques
 I. Title
 751.42′2432

ISBN 0 00 412343 3

Printed and bound in Italy
by New Interlitho SpA, Milan

CONTENTS

PORTRAIT OF AN ARTIST
PETER PARTINGTON

Fig. 1 Peter Partington sketching birds near his home

Peter Partington was born in Cambridge in 1941. Apart from one idyllic year on a farm in Suffolk after the war, most of his early childhood was spent in the London suburbs. When he was eleven his family moved to Poole in Dorset and this proved to be one of the formative influences on his teenage years. His love of landscape and wildlife was stimulated by the ever changing light on the landlocked sea of Poole Harbour, sheltered by the hills of Purbeck.

His early artistic efforts encouraged him to study painting, drawing and printmaking at Bournemouth College of Art. While he was there he became deeply interested in abstract art, which he feels gave him a keen insight into colour, design, form and texture. After leaving college he gained his Art Teacher's Certificate at Hornsey (now Middlesex) College of Art, and then for a period of almost twenty years he taught painting and drawing full-time to art students. He is now a freelance artist and illustrator.

His profound knowledge of birds lends additional weight to the text and illustrations in this book. He began watching birds at the age of fourteen and started painting them and the surrounding landscape he loved long before his college days. Poole Harbour was a stone's throw from school, so it was easy to slip across the railway embankment and spend lunchtimes watching and drawing birds on the shore. Holidays and weekends were an excuse to range the hidden backwaters of the harbour, as well as to venture by cycle to Swanage, Wareham and Portland Bill to experience the cliff-birds and explore the streams and woods of deep Dorset.

From the start he was attracted to the work of those artists who, like the Chinese and Japanese, sought to capture spirit and atmosphere, rather than exactitude. Sharp observation and vivid brushwork drew him to the work of artists like Southgate, Scott, Tunnicliffe, Ennion and Talbot Kelly, all of whom he would recommend to the aspiring art student for further study.

Peter Partington's own work is definitely not of the 'minutely particular' variety. He loves the broad freedom of the watercolour wash and the concomitant discipline needed to control it. He attempts to capture the light, the moods of the moment when we experience the animal in its world. To him the bird and its habitat, whether it be a summer sky or a few wet pebbles, are inseparable. This calls for an immediate impressionistic grasp of the total vision.

Peter Partington has become recognized as a leading exponent of watercolour and as an artist who depicts birds and animals in their environment with insight, knowledge and authenticity. In 1985 he was elected a member of the Society of Wildlife Artists, and now serves on the committee. He is listed in *Who's Who in Art*.

He has had a succession of one-man shows at important galleries throughout Britain. His paintings are eagerly collected and often reproduced for calendars, magazines and prints. He has painted for the prestigious cover of the RSPB's magazine *Birds* and recently he undertook the major task of illustrating *Down the River,* H. E. Bates's semi-autobiography. His work for this has been much acclaimed. In addition, he has his own etching studio where he prints editions of his internationally successful wildlife prints.

It gave him much pleasure to realize that by writing this book he is spreading the idea of conservation. If artists are encouraged to appreciate and express the vitality of bird-life and habitat, the birds and the countryside will have that many more friends and allies. He himself is a keen supporter and life member of the Royal Society for the Protection of Birds.

Peter Partington now lives in North Kent with his wife and three grown-up children. His tall house is high on a hill and looks down on the Thames estuary. From his studio he can see the marshes and countryside he loves to depict and where he watches birds. The river, with its busy traffic and Essex shore opposite, is a never failing source of interest.

Fig. 2 *Little Terns, Minsmere,* 1985

WHY PAINT BIRDS?

Bird-life is a source of wonder and satisfaction to all of us. I remember the thrill I had when I spotted my first goldfinch at the age of fourteen. Last winter, and somewhat older now, I was overcome by the flickering vision of at least two hundred of these chequered beauties feeding on the fluffy lane-side thistles on the marshes near my home in Kent. I haven't attempted to paint the scene yet!

A spectacle like that is pure delight; but of course birds offer us even more than visual pleasure. They invest our landscape, from wilderness to suburb, with life, colour and music. With romance, too – like the peregrine falcon which chooses the high crags and inaccessible cliffs for its home; which lives the life of a wild and independent hunter, and which flies like the wind. The grouse and the ptarmigan earn our respect for their life on high mountain tops, enduring the arctic winters. The songs and habits of the thrushes, the robins and the finches of our suburbs and gardens are woven into our everyday affections.

Above all our imagination is fired by their great migrations. The vast journeys made by the skeins of geese from the far north to reach Britain in winter demand our admiration. We eagerly await the first cuckoo, and the warblers, which reassure us with their song that summer might just be on its way. We are amazed that such scraps of vitality can navigate and fly enormous distances to return each year to our hedges and gardens.

Artists have found in these things a source of endless inspiration. They certainly inspire me and I hope that in this book I can convey something of the enjoyment, the satisfaction and the experience I have had in painting birds, to encourage you to do likewise.

Many of you may have quite a lot of experience in painting landscape and similar subjects in watercolour. Perhaps you opened this book wondering at first if there were any useful tips in it you haven't yet picked up. You may also have pondered at times how you might integrate birds into your work, either as a

Fig. 3 Goldfinches, Cliffe Marshes, Kent

point of focus or to enliven a sky with a flying bird. In this case the notes on birds in flight should be useful (see page 32). Putting a bird into a landscape requires some knowledge: the bird needs to look authentic in terms of the species, and the scale, colour and lighting must be correct. I hope I can be of help here, too, and that you will find some stimulating ideas in the text that might invite you to turn your vision and craft towards the bird world.

On the other hand, you may be a knowledgeable and keen bird-watcher wishing to develop a more lively and personal record of a day's birding. The notes on bird shape and using a sketchbook will be useful to you (see pages 24 and 38). Working through the other exercises in this book will help you progress to more ambitious painting projects.

But what about absolute beginners? Where do they begin? I hope this book will provide the answers to these questions by explaining how to go about collecting information and ideas with your sketchbook; describing what you need to know about the anatomy and the character of birds; and then showing how to commit that knowledge to paper with brushwork, tone and colour.

The first question I'm inevitably asked by beginners is, 'How on earth can you paint birds...they're so quick in their movements; they don't wait around to be sketched, let alone painted?' And, it must be admitted, there is a lot of truth in this. The small birds, like the warblers, are often gone in seconds, or are so mobile that they present a constantly changing pattern and form. It is for this reason that I stress in this book the importance of the sketchbook, the practice of brushwork, and the development of informed memorizing. However, some of the smaller birds, like the song thrush, will sit still for some time, especially in cold weather or after a good meal. On a hot day, a blackbird will sun itself for twenty minutes in the flowerbed, its wings spread in heraldic patterns.

The larger birds are more accessible than you might think. A heron, for example, is motionless as it stalks a fish, so there is plenty of time to draw it. The stately crane family walk with measured dignity and grace. Pheasants and partridges will often 'freeze' when suspicious before they explode into take-off.

If you watch birds feeding at a bird-table you will find they continuously adopt similar attitudes and poses. This means you can start a sketch and come back to it later if necessary. Your growing knowledge of feathers and anatomy will enable you to complete some sketches at your leisure.

There is other assistance at hand, too, to enable you to study birds more easily and at close quarters. You can watch tame birds and make visits to bird parks, aviaries, zoos and farmyards. Very good views of wild birds can be had from hides at nature reserves. And, of course, you can use a camera, an essential piece of equipment, to capture still images of birds (of which more later).

As for freshness and originality in your work, there is only one way to achieve this and that is to use your eyes. Go out, observe, and observe again and again. I can promise you many hours of sheer pleasure. You will not be out there simply to 'tick' birds neurotically into a notebook, as some bird-watchers do, but to enjoy a bird's life and share imaginatively in its existence. You can admire the subtlety of its camouflage, or its bold display plumage; you can savour the pattern of leaves around it, or its reflections in a pebbly pool. Last winter, for example, I noticed this blackcap (**fig. 4**) in our garden feeding from ivy berries. It was a surprise; they usually visit us in summer. It posed and stretched to reach the berries with all the delicacy of an exercising ballerina. It returned several times and these sketches are a compilation of my observations.

There is always the additional excitement of lively incidents, like crows mobbing a hen harrier (what flying!); lapwings leading you from the nest by feigning injury; or mistle thrushes defending their nest against magpies. All this fascinating bird-life is there to be enjoyed and loved. To illustrate this, let me describe to you three contrasting field trips I enjoyed last year.

Fig. 4 Blackcap

A walk on the marshes

The first trip was to the south coast, looking from Lymington over the Solent towards the Isle of Wight. After a frosty start, the day was clear and warm by mid-morning. I parked the car on a knoll by the pasture behind the sea wall. The distant hills of the Isle were pale, the straits were silver and the sunlight golden. In the distance a heron flew slowly along the sea wall, while a magpie, oblivious of the car, perched nearby, strongly lit, in an interesting tree. I drew the magpie for a minute or two. It skimmed away when I got out of the car.

I took the long path west to Keyhaven, enjoying the warmth of the day and the colours of dried reed, scarlet hawthorn berries, and the fresh green of sodden pasture. There were peewits calling and yellowhammers 'chipping'. As I scrambled to the crest of the vast sea defences that lead out to Hurst Castle, skeins of black brent geese were flying up offshore to a mere which I could see in the distance. This area was hardly a wilderness (houses surrounded most of it) yet on this stretch of water was the largest collection of brent geese I had ever seen – at least five hundred of them, perhaps more. This was an exciting start to the day.

The lake was bordered by a footpath and I found a place to sit quietly and took out my sketchbook. The brent geese were resting, preening and bickering occasionally. After ten minutes the flock took spectacular flight, with a cacophony of sound. After a flight round, wave after wave glided in, long wings outspread, side-slipping and skidding to rest on the water. It gave me many useful sketches of the birds taking flight and landing. As I began to walk back eastwards along the shore the geese were still conducting thrilling fly-pasts against the sun along the shore. What pictures were here!

The twists and turns of the shoreline presented ever changing variations of light and colour. To the west the hills and sea were bleached with mist and light. To the east the sea assumed a line of pure ultramarine in the warm grey distance and below pale cobalt blue hills. Between were all the variations of colour you might expect. The sand and grass were bright against the sea. I sat and painted this scene, for no other reason than that I enjoyed the contrasts of tone and colour, as well as the sun's warmth and smell of the shore.

Afterwards I picked myself up, rounded the point, and spotted the hunched form of a heron digesting a meal out on the saltings. Its pastel grey plumage was lit up against the deep green-browns of a mud bank. The heron moved only slightly and I had plenty of time to check my sketches and make several attempts.

The day was more advanced now – and the sunlight picked out every blade of grass. I noted a small bay ahead with some waders feeding, so I took bearings and

Fig. 5 Brent geese

moved up in the shelter of the sea wall. I carefully emerged among the tussocks without disturbing the birds and trained my binoculars into the bay. Wonderful scenes greeted my eyes: grey and ringed plover were reflected in the sky-blue pools; little parties of dunlin were retreating delicately before the tide, feeding busily. They occupied each reedy hummock of mud until it was obliterated by the brimming water.

There was scope for a dozen watercolours there. I made some notes, but there was hardly time to sketch, only to absorb, to commit the light, colour and atmosphere to memory. I sometimes find myself mentally going through the motions of using a paint brush and colour when faced with scenes like this; it helps.

The day ended with an astounding sunset. All varieties of blues, bronzes and greens from the hills were reflected in the water. A great crested grebe swam along the shore, contributing its ripples to the kaleidoscope. Last but not least of the day's birds was a kingfisher on the shore, drowsing idly on a twiggy piece of driftwood. All the colours of the evening were concentrated in its plumage.

Fig. 6 Dunlin

Watching black grouse

The second trip, to mid-Wales in spring, was very different. I had been determined for some time to watch the display and mating ceremony of the black grouse. A fellow bird artist and friend in that area had made enquiries and found a 'lek', which is the small area adopted by the grouse to forgather. Here the cocks show off and spar with one another. The females choose a mate, usually the dominant male who has fought off the others and occupies the central territory. The ceremonies take place in the morning and evening.

This trip entailed some organization. First we had to pinpoint the lek from the road. Once we'd done this, we borrowed a hide and erected it the next day, camouflaging it carefully. This now had to be left for a day or two so the birds could get used to it, so in the meantime we had fun in the mountains looking for red kites and pied flycatchers. I also visited that wonderful RSPB reserve Ynys-Hir . . . that's another tale!

On the appointed morning we arrived before dawn and under cover of darkness crawled into the hide. We

Fig. 7 Black grouse

Fig. 8 The black grouse 'lek'

kept very still until we were quite sure the birds did not suspect our presence. We could hear that they were already there; their sound was a sort of vibration interspersed with excited bubbling noises. The first light lifted itself over the mountains and we began to discern the black shapes of the cock birds, with their white lacy under-tail coverts fluffed over their behinds, while the extraordinary scimitars of their extended tails curved forwards round their wings, which were lowered pugnaciously.

Never before had it been so apparent to me how volatile is the form of a bird, how quickly it can arrange its feather masses to change its shape so that it is almost unrecognizable. The late males flew in as precise and streamlined shapes. As they caught the excitement they puffed their gun-metal blue neck feathers into bull necks, lifted their tails high, and raised their fluffy white underwear. From the side they could appear as round as footballs: from the front they resembled nothing so much as enormous old-fashioned black telephone receivers, an effect heightened by the deep black of their plumage. They became an abstract design in black and white, topped by crimson wattles, mulberry-like, stuck over their eyebrows, which were now catching the sun's rays. All the while they were jousting and bouncing each other in mock boxing; a few feathers flew, but there were no injuries.

We drew feverishly, but at the same time tried to absorb and enjoy the spectacle, and to take in the spirit of the place.

As the amber daylight spread up the valley it highlighted more of the birds' plumage. But now the ceremonies began to dissolve, the crowd dispersed, and the party drew to a close. All that was left to us was a sunlit but featureless field by the edge of a young pine plantation. But what magic while it lasted!

In the orchard

You don't have to travel far to find birds. I am quite happy to watch sparrows and starlings on the lawn, and greenfinches and collared doves on the bird-table. My third trip was really only a summery afternoon in a friend's garden but very relaxing!

The hammock was set up in the orchard and I lay back with my sketchbook, watching the poultry as they foraged amongst the leaves and grass. I threw them a few handfuls of grain to keep them from wandering.

I enjoyed the shapes of the hens as they clucked around – tails quite pointed and roof-like from behind and wedge-shaped from the side. It was the simple contrast of black and white that attracted me to the two resting hens (**fig. 9**). The black hen reflected some blue in its plumage from the summer sky. The white hen was

10

formed by painting the foliage around its shape and leaving the white area untouched. I remembered to brush in some pale green where the feathers reflected the colour of foliage.

I like making up sketchbook pages – they can carry a great deal of lively information (**fig. 10**). Here I used a

Fig. 9 Resting hens

pencil line to define the shapes quickly and added colour washes to note the plumages. Tinted paper is attractive and particularly useful for beginners as it provides some ready-made colour to work into.

The cockerel was a magnificent creature, a Leghorn type with a sensational plumage – orange-yellow nape, purple wings, and a lustrous bottle-green tail fluttering like pennants in the wind. It was then, I think, that I first noticed that these pennants are in fact the upper-tail coverts supported by the actual tail. The cockerel's wattles shone like poppies in the sun and the glancing sunlight in the orchard enhanced its shot-silk plumage. Other breeds were busy here, too, such as Bantams of different sorts, living their almost natural lives among the weeds and grass.

There are, of course, many days that aren't as delightful or action-packed as these – days when it's too wet to draw, or when however hard you search there isn't a bird in sight. But these are more than made up for by those other lovely days. My aim here is to show you how you can now make an exciting visual record of them.

Fig. 10 Sketches of poultry

WHAT EQUIPMENT DO YOU NEED?

Fig. 11 A selection of materials for painting in watercolour

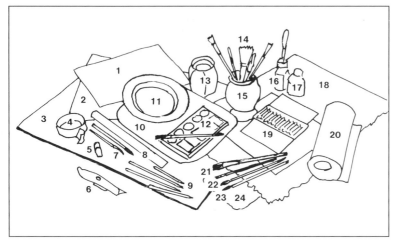

1 Layout pad
2 Cartridge pad
3 Drawing board
4 Masking tape
5 Eraser
6 Stanley knife
7 Pens
8 Ruler
9 Pencils
10 Plastic palette
11 Tin palette
12 China palette
13 Water pot
14 Brushes
15 Brush pot
16 Ox-gall solution
17 Masking fluid
18 Watercolour paper
19 Paint box with tubes
   of watercolour
20 Kitchen paper
21 Square-tipped
   brushes
22 Sable brush
23 Liner brush
24 Blotting paper

Those of you who have had some experience of watercolour painting will probably have found brushes, colours and papers that suit you already, but those new to bird painting may find some additional helpful information here relating specifically to this subject. Complete beginners will find useful guidelines about materials and equipment which will enable them to walk confidently into an art supply shop and discuss with the dealer what they need.

Watercolours

It is always advisable to buy the best-quality materials. Without any doubt Artists' Quality Watercolours are by far and away the best – but, of course, they can be expensive. Georgian Watercolours provide the leisure painter and student with high-quality paints at a lower price. You can learn all you want to know about watercolour with these if you wish.

Both Georgian and Artists' colours can be bought in a box complete with pans or half pans. Artists' colours are also available in quarter pans. Pans are hard lozenges of paint which dissolve under the action of a wet brush. Watercolour paint also comes in tubes and if you prefer you can purchase an empty box and fill it with the colours of your choice. Tubes are really more useful in the studio when you are working on more ambitious pictures as larger quantities of colour are needed quickly to mix washes for bigger areas of paper. These tubes of paint can be placed at the ready. I have demonstrated some of the colours available – my own personal choice – in **fig. 14** on page 16.

Brushes

The price and the quality of brushes vary greatly. The very best brushes are those made from Kolinsky sable (Diana Series). They are also the most expensive. I prize one of these wonderful brushes myself, a No. 14. It is responsive and yet firm, and it holds an enormous quantity of wash. Other, less expensive, real-hair brushes are also available, those made of red sable being next in quality, then squirrel and ox-hair. All these brushes function very adequately. You will gradually discover which brushes suit your style and your purse; for instance, I enjoy using the wide range of inexpensive, synthetic brushes in the Dalon series.

You need a versatile full-bodied brush that makes a fine point for large, expressive work, such as a Dalon

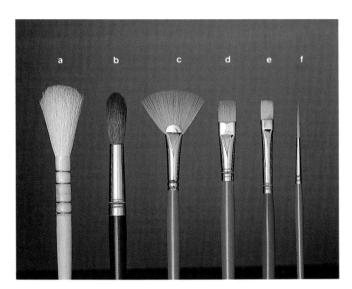

a   Series 34G mop brush No. 4
b   Series 40 Kolinsky sable brush No. 14
c   Series D55 fan-shaped brush No. 6
d   Series D44 square-tipped brush No. 10
e   Series 280 white nylon brush No. 6
f   Series D99 'liner' brush No. 3

Fig. 12 A selection of brushes

Series D77 No. 14, and a range of smaller brushes. A big mop brush, like the Series 34G, is good for laying on big areas of water. By contrast I use a Dalon Series D99 No. 2 'rigger' or 'liner' brush for preliminary drawing. I also find a fan-shaped hog bristle brush useful.

Less often employed for watercolour but very useful for bird painting are the square-tipped brushes. I have found various sizes of the Dalon Series D22, D44, or the soft hair Series 55 to be ideal. I also find that some of the pure nylon bristle brushes, such as the Series 280, when used in conjunction with water and blotting paper, are excellent for erasing areas of colour.

Some of my older brushes have developed strange shapes and lost their hair – but they all have their uses for painting twigs or fur or feathers. Hang on to yours; try them out and see what marks they make. For further information about the various effects that can be achieved by different brushes, see the section on brushwork (page 20).

Eventually you will discover what brushes you can work with most easily and no doubt will add to the number of unexpectedly useful ones.

Paper

Watercolour paper is manufactured in a range of thicknesses which are described by weight (lb), by ream, or by grams per square metre (gsm). Paper is produced in three surface textures: HP (hot-pressed), Not (which stands for not hot-pressed) and Rough. HP paper has the smoothest texture; Not paper lies somewhere between HP and Rough and is the surface I find most conducive for bird painting. It is smooth enough to register detail, but textured enough to catch that sparkling watercolour wash texture. Rough paper is too textured for the detail required for birds.

I try to avoid the chore of stretching the paper so my choice of weight is determined by the maximum size which will not buckle when a wash is applied. For instance, a piece of unstretched 90 lb (185 gsm) Whatman paper (Not surface) will buckle if it is any larger than A5 size (21×14.5 cm or 8¼×5¾ in). Therefore, for me, the larger the work, the heavier the paper should be. An Imperial size piece of 300 lb (638 gsm) Saunders Waterford series paper – a thick, heavy paper – will buckle only a little even when thoroughly doused with water.

The price of watercolour paper varies according to weight and also according to how much wood fibre, as opposed to cotton fibre, it contains. It is the cotton fibre that gives Waterford or Whatman such strength. Bockingford is composed of wood fibre, but it is a good, strong, inexpensive paper for the beginner. It is 'acid free', which means it has been chemically treated to prevent it eventually turning brown – a useful assurance for a would-be purchaser of your work. With practice you will soon discover the paper that is most congenial to you.

Other useful equipment

There are a number of other items that you will need in your studio. Palettes are essential for mixing colour; I have two plastic trays which are ideal for mixing large quantities of wash, and for smaller amounts of colour I use white tin plates. You can buy white china palettes with five round and five slanting wells. Near to hand I keep masking tape, masking fluid, ox-gall solution (which is used for colour blending and to prevent pigment spreading too much in a wash), blotting paper, a ruler, eraser, a couple of water pots (jam jars), pens, pencils ranging from HB to 4B, and some Stanley blades for sharpening them. In addition, I have a layout pad (30×20 cm/12×8 in), some cartridge paper for sketching out, planning compositions and testing colour, and a roll of kitchen paper for emergencies. I have a variety of drawing boards of different sizes – the largest of which can take Imperial-sized paper (76×56 cm/30×22 in) – which are made of three-ply wood – light enough for manoeuvrability. A heavy board is an encumbrance because you need to be able to turn a board freely for some effects.

My desk is tilted and wide enough to spread out sketchbooks on it. In front of it I have a pinboard which is very useful for pinning up sketches and roughs from which I am working. Behind the desk are shelves of reference material I have collected over the years. There is almost too much of it, in fact; I find myself referring to only a fairly limited selection of books for plumage details, and so on. Information derived from on-the-spot observation is the best kind of all.

Equipment for field trips

At home or in the studio you have the space and time to employ a wide range of materials, as already described. For field trips, when you are exploring a nature reserve or following a coastal footpath, watching birds and gathering information, it is best to reduce your kit to essentials: just enough equipment to work for you, but not too much to weigh you down and make the day hard-going. So for a successful day out a little planning and rationalization of your equipment is a must.

I keep all my basic equipment in a small fishing tackle bag, ready at a moment's notice (**fig. 13**). This includes a pocket paint box and brushes, a small hardback sketchbook and 6B pencils, a retractable knife or pencil sharpener, an eraser, blotting paper, a water bottle, and two special items of equipment for bird painting – a pair of binoculars and a camera with a zoom lens.

The paint box must be small and easily portable. Some types incorporate their own water carrier and container as well as a collapsible brush and small pans of paint, and these are ideal. For convenience the sketchbook need be no larger than A5 (21×14.5 cm/ 8¼×5¾ in). Daler-Rowney's small hardback sketchbook contains ivory-coloured paper which I find very sympathetic and which will take a wash or two of watercolour.

My binoculars are 10×50 – fairly powerful – and they are a bit heavy. Many of you may prefer lighter binoculars. There is much advice available to you about suitable binoculars in magazines on bird-watching. The camera that I use is an SLR with through-lens light meter, and I have a telephoto 70–210 mm zoom lens for 'framing' my shots. I find colour print film at 200 ASA quite adequate for daylight photography, and the advantage of prints is that they make for easy reference.

I store the camera in the bag's main section, which is lined with foam rubber. In the adjacent zipped section I stow the sketchbook and pencils, the knife or sharpener and eraser, where I can get at them easily. In the outside pocket I keep two rolls of spare film and any other oddments that might come in handy – like plastic bags for collecting dead birds. I keep some blotting paper, the watercolour box and the water bottle, which I use for mixing colour and washing brushes, in the nearside compartment. All this equipment fits easily into the front of the car and I can set off with the assurance that I have all the tools I need to bring back a record of the day's events to the studio.

For an extended trip, perhaps if you wish to study landscape and habitats or observe a single species in greater depth, more equipment can be deployed. For observation purposes you may decide to use a hide, although I find my car makes an excellent moving hide – the birds do not seem to mind it. I keep my binoculars at the ready on the front seat and often paint from the car if it's raining. Remember to keep an eye on the rear-view mirror before stopping suddenly, however.

When sallying forth to paint habitat – whether it be a mountainside or just a few brambles – you can revert to more orthodox methods. Take with you a tubular folding seat (others tend to sink in soft ground) and a folding easel – there are numerous types of these available, but make sure you choose one that is able to hold your work horizontally to enable you to apply colour washes. For this kind of outdoor work watercolour pads and blocks are useful. The latter contain sheets of ready-prepared stretched watercolour paper and are available in various weights and sizes. You simply remove the upper sheet of paper when your painting is completed. I recommend you take two of these blocks so that you can work on another picture while washes are drying on the first. Alternatively, you could take your drawing board with you and some larger sheets of

Fig. 13 Basic equipment for field trips

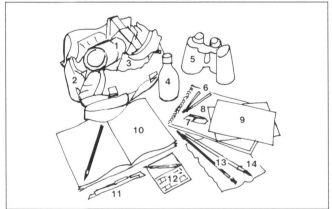

1 Camera with zoom lens
2 Fishing tackle bag
3 Plastic bag
4 Water bottle
5 Binoculars
6 Pencils
7 Eraser
8 Watercolour pad
9 Watercolour blocks
10 Hardback sketchbook
11 Knife with retractable blade
12 Pocket paint box with brush
13 Brushes
14 Blotting paper

paper, plus perhaps a larger paint box and a wider range of brushes; but choose your equipment carefully, as you may have to carry it for some distance. Again, keep your binoculars ready – the quiet activity of the 'plein-air' painter doesn't seem to disturb the birds. I once paused for several minutes to watch a sparrowhawk which landed close by. I made a quick sketch of it and then got on with my painting.

Lastly, give some thought to your personal comfort. In winter, wear plenty of warm clothing and if you paint in the snow, stand on a thick wad of newspaper. In summer, wear a light hat. A packet of nuts and raisins slipped into the pocket of my jacket usually keeps me going foodwise.

If you have worked outdoors in watercolour before, much of this equipment will be familiar to you. I cannot underline enough, however, the importance of keeping such a kit near you wherever you may be. You won't regret the lively work that occurs when painting in situ.

USING COLOUR

Let me show you briefly some of the colours I enjoy using. This is a personal selection; I hope you will go on to experiment, to add to them, and discover the colours that suit you.

In **fig. 14** I dragged a wet brush over the paper and fed into it blues, yellows and reds, ranging from warm tones on the left to cool ones on the right. Below these are three earth colours. The last one, Yellow Ochre, is a favourite colour of mine, one which always seems to suggest sunshine. All these colours can be mixed in varying proportions and with different amounts of water to produce an infinite number of colours and tones. The deepest tone available from these colours is my substitute for black. I rarely use black straight from the marked tube, although some artists enjoy the effects of colour that the addition of black can produce. Instead I mix up a strong combination of Burnt Umber and Permanent Blue to create a 'living' black full of resonance and depth. As you can see from the examples at the bottom of **fig. 14**, this can be tipped towards warmth or coolness. Try it.

Fig. 15 illustrates a few of the greens available. Understanding green is essential if you are looking at birds in landscapes, or indeed at specific birds such as a greenfinch or a peacock. In the centre I painted a base colour of Sap Green. I then added to this in the outside ring the colours already illustrated above and reversed some of these in the inner ring to show how colours can 'sing' when warm ones are placed against cold. You can say goodbye forever to stale vegetable greens in your foliage!

The brighter yellow-greens and blue-greens I find especially useful for portraying sunlight and shadow, the Yellow Ochre green for sunlight through leaves, and the Burnt Umber green for the depths of undergrowth. Of course, with the addition of more water to your wash, you can further widen the range and increase the subtlety of your colours.

One of the loveliest and subtlest colours nature gives us is the grey of clouds, from the deep and stormy to the light and fluffy of a summer's day. This 'natural' grey can be made up from Permanent Blue, Yellow Ochre and a touch of Cadmium Red. In **fig. 16** there are three variations from blue-grey to brown-grey. It is worth playing around with the possible variations of this delightful and uplifting range of greys.

Some brief examples of how colour can be intensified by the addition of small and contrasting areas of colour are also shown in **fig. 16**. One has only to think of poppies or chicory flowers in hayfields to

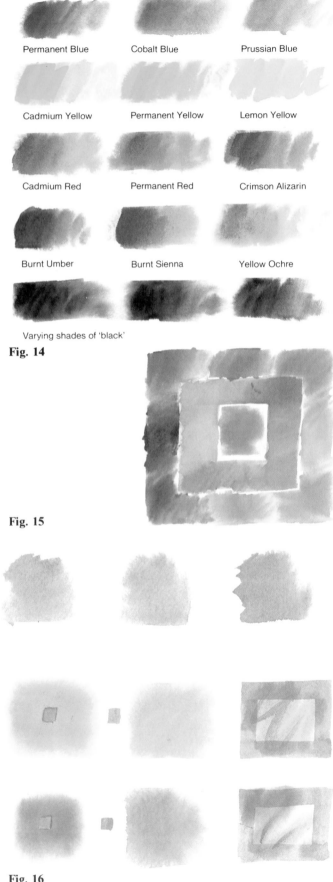

Permanent Blue   Cobalt Blue   Prussian Blue

Cadmium Yellow   Permanent Yellow   Lemon Yellow

Cadmium Red   Permanent Red   Crimson Alizarin

Burnt Umber   Burnt Sienna   Yellow Ochre

Varying shades of 'black'

Fig. 14

Fig. 15

Fig. 16

realize how the green or ochre base colour is intensified by the colours of the individual scarlet blobs of the poppies or the blue scraps of the chicory.

Figs. 17–19 show how some of these principles can be applied in a painting.

In landscape painting the blues always suggest distance; the cooler and paler the blues used the greater this feeling of distance becomes. The peacock in **fig. 17** is doubly exciting, therefore, in that the bird displays its gorgeous and varied blues very close to us.

For this study, composed entirely from a range of blues, I first washed in a pale Permanent Blue for the sky and a pale wash of Prussian Blue for the distant hills, with Cobalt Blue for the nearer ones. I then worked into the bird's neck area with a pale Prussian Blue and while it was wet fed in a strong mix of Permanent Blue around the edges and on the head. This set up the cool-warm contrast which can at times seem visually to vibrate. When this was dry, using a liner brush I flicked in a suggestion of feathers in Cobalt Blue, followed by an overpainting of deeper Permanent Blue on the head and eye.

In the painting of feeding starlings I wanted to suggest the feel of deep summer (**fig. 18**). The area is underpainted with a Yellow Ochre wash tinted with Crimson Alizarin at the 'back'. While this was still damp, I fed into it yellow-green for sunlit patches and blue-green for shadow. I then allowed the resulting soft image to dry. The detail of the hedge was achieved by working into it with heavy greens, particularly Sap Green mixed with Burnt Umber. I used a stiff brush to scrub back some light into the hedge top.

Starlings are glossy, so here they appear very black in the blue-green shadows and quite bright in the sunshine. I strengthened the Crimson Alizarin slightly in the background and used touches of the same colour in greater strength on the foreground weeds. This further enlivened the greens.

In the picture of red-legged partridge, or 'Frenchmen' as they are sometimes called (**fig. 19**), I began by masking out the flower shapes. (This technique is dealt with in more detail on page 19.) I washed a pale mix of Yellow Ochre over the picture area and when that dried I drew in the shapes of the birds with a liner brush. I then picked these out by adding deeper colour around them, a greyer version of the Yellow Ochre. I wanted to create a feeling of reflected light, so I left their flank feathers fairly pale.

When all this was dry I rubbed out the mask from the flowers and painted in their colours. I emphasized the scarlet of the birds' eyelids and beaks, rather than the poppies, to draw attention to their heads. Their splendidly graphic head markings helped here, too. The various patches of bright colour illustrate well how the passive Yellow Ochre ground can be heightened and yet still retain its control over all the different colours.

Fig. 17 Peacock, painted entirely from a range of blues

Fig. 18 A mixture of different greens creates a vibrant effect

Fig. 19 Patches of bright colour intensify a background

BASIC TECHNIQUES

Laying a wash

To lay a sparkling veil of colour down on a chunky piece of Not surface watercolour paper with a wash of watercolour is a magical experience. Watercolour has an infinite capacity to capture light, texture and movement. It can summon up reflected sunlight, translucent shadows; and especially, as if like called to like, reflections, ripples and texture in lakes, streams and seas.

If you are like me and even a pencil in the hand makes you itch to draw, then tubes of colour, a pot of brushes, a huge jar of sparkling fresh water, and a pad of Not paper will cause whole afternoons and days to disappear just like that – but with lots of paintings to show for them!

However, newcomers to the medium might eye their newly purchased watercolour boxes and shiny brushes with some trepidation. Well, the longest journey begins, as the Chinese say, with the first step – so, make it easy for yourself. Start by setting up your painting table with some thought. If you are right-handed, put all your equipment on the right of your painting point. Have your selection of brushes in a pot nearby. Fill up two jars of water, one for washing brushes, the other for adding to your colours. Place in front of these your palettes and dishes. Make sure you have some masking fluid and ox-gall liquid to hand. You will also need blotting paper for accidents and alterations, and a roll of kitchen paper ready for emergencies.

Cut down your paper to a size that suits you, while bearing in mind that watercolour washes are always easier to handle over small areas. Fix the paper firmly to your board with masking tape. As I have mentioned before I am not a great enthusiast of all the activity that goes with stretching paper, such as soaking it in the bath and sticking it down with gum strip. If I need a larger piece of paper I use a good thick one (300 lb/ 638 gsm) which will not cockle when wetted.

All is now ready. Squeeze out small amounts of the colours you want from the tubes onto your palette; soak your brush and mix some colour with it to form a pool. The first secret of successful watercolouring is always to dissolve the colour completely and evenly in the water to form the wash. The second is to use the brush, fully charged with wash whenever you can, to maintain flow. Remember to let the water do as much of the work for you as it can.

In the first study here (**fig. 20**) I used the blues, ochres and cloud greys that I have already talked about. I wetted the paper (Not surface, 140 lb/300 gsm) and then

Fig. 20 First stage of a wash

Fig. 21 Completed wash

with a Series 28 16 mm (⅝ in) brush added a Yellow Ochre wash into the lower half, strengthening it slightly towards the bottom. This was to create warmth. I dried this with my hair dryer – a useful way of speeding up the drying process – and then redamped the area with clean water. Into this damp base I dabbed and streaked some grey cloud shapes with a flat brush. I deepened the grey towards the 'horizon'. You can see how effective it is in watercolour when you work from light to dark. When you try this exercise, to prevent the clouds spreading too widely, add a little ox-gall liquid when you mix the colour. If you haven't used watercolours before, try this exercise over and over again; you will soon get the hang of it.

Big cumulus clouds possess hard edges at their summits and are softer below. For this reason in **fig. 21** I redamped just the lower half of the picture. Then, after mixing a wash of Permanent Blue, I took a brushful and worked down around the cloud shapes. I gradually added Prussian Blue as I continued and met the damp area, where this colour merged softly. I added a streak of Prussian Blue lower in the sky and put in the blue-green hills, which were hardly stronger than the clouds. A buzzard seemed then to find its way into the sky!

Using masking fluid

If you need to work fairly precisely, your technique can be enhanced by the use of masking fluid. This substance is a sort of rubbery glue which is waterproof when dry. It is used to mask out certain parts of a painting to enable a wash to be applied over the whole area without restriction. It is then rubbed away, leaving clearly defined areas to be painted.

There are a few important rules you should follow when using masking fluid. Always wash out your brush immediately after using it to apply the fluid. Always make sure your paper is bone dry before applying masking fluid and before using an eraser to rub it off. I can testify to a few ruined brushes and painting failures simply through having overlooked these rules in the excitement of creativity.

In this study of quail and pineapple weed (**fig. 22**), I began by masking out the petals using a thin brush as, of course, they were to remain white. After the masking fluid had dried I painted over them with a wash of pale Yellow Ochre. I added a pale wash of Cobalt Blue to indicate the position of the quail. The quail is basically a buff-coloured bird, so I waited for the Yellow Ochre to dry and then masked out the bird's shape on this colour. This I then dried.

I rewetted the area and fed in a yellow-green to suggest leaves and some Burnt Umber for depth and shadow under the bird and the plant. I let all this dry thoroughly and then removed the mask with a stiff eraser. I washed in a pale Cobalt Blue to create shadow on some of the petals and put in the flower centres with Permanent Yellow. With a fine Dalon Series D99 No. 2

Fig. 22 Stages of a painting using masking fluid

brush I painted in the streaks and blotches of the bird's plumage with masking fluid, allowing this to dry before working further into the feathers. When the painting was dry I rubbed off the mask.

I based the quail and the pineapple weed on sketches in my sketchbook, but I referred to photographs for the final details of the quail's plumage.

Brushwork

Already, I expect, you may have gathered some hints on brushwork – like the importance of a full brush and of flow, as well as devices like dragging a brush over textured paper. Every artist has his or her favourite brushes but there are certain types which produce effects that are remarkably useful for the bird artist.

The 'liner' or 'rigger' brush, like the Daler-Rowney Series D99 No. 3 or 4, for example, can produce fine, rhythmic lines and is ideal either for its own sake or for preparatory sketching-in. Used freely from the wrist, the brush has a 'spring' and a 'whippiness' to it that enables you to produce exciting lines. This is ideal for grasses and twigs, and imparts a rhythm and liveliness to bird outlines as well. I have used it here (**fig. 23**) for practice strokes and to make a quick drawing of a swan and water rail. You will enjoy using this brush.

Another useful brush is the square-tipped flat brush, which produces a variety of marks, as the next few

Fig. 23 Swan and water rail, sketched with a 'liner' brush

Fig. 24 Gyrfalcon, drawn with a square-tipped brush

Fig. 25

examples show. Horizontal strokes can be used to create ripples in perspective, and verticals can suggest reflections and water surface. One of this brush's enormous virtues is the way it can depict feathering in plumage (see also page 23).

At the top of **fig. 24** I have demonstrated some brush exercises you can experiment with, using various sizes of square-tipped brushes from Daler-Rowney's Series 133 or Dalon D88. If you hold your brush at various angles and use different wrist movements you can produce attractive patterns of thick and thin strokes. These patterns can depict the complexity of plumage and allow you to build up the impression of feathering quickly and easily.

A quick flicking stroke produces a perspective effect as well as indicating an individual feather. It enables you to 'wrap' these 'feathers' around the bird, as you can see in the study of the gyrfalcon opposite.

Other movements and angles can suggest the fall of the breast feathers and their individual marks. If you try to capture the spiral quality that underlies feathering, you will give your bird a sense of roundness.

The scene with a swimming cormorant (**fig. 25**) was painted entirely with a square-tipped brush. The ripples were formed with a horizontal wrist action, while the stump and its reflection were made with a vertical

flat stroke. The depth of water was suggested by vertical strokes of deepening colour worked into a damped area of the paper.

I keep one or two oddities in my brush pot. For example, a hog's-hair 'fan', Daler-Rowney Series B84, is ideal for creating those scribbly types of reflections among grasses. A nylon brush can be very effective for scrubbing out colour from the paper surface. I use this in conjunction with blotting paper and lots of clean water. Watercolourists have traditionally used knives to scrape and prick back to the white paper for highlights; my nylon brush is a useful extension to the armoury.

Watercolour lends itself to liquid spontaneous brushwork which is why it gives so much satisfaction. **Figs. 26–8** illustrate some further examples of brushwork which you may enjoy experimenting with. For the tuft of grass in **fig. 26** I used a Dalon Series D77 No. 7 brush, allowing a Yellow Ochre wash to spread into brush strokes of clean water that I had already laid down. While this was still damp I added a strong bluegrey to the base of the shape to suggest shadow. Remember that strong colour will always blend easily into a weaker wash.

Next I folded a small piece of blotting paper and with this edge took out a few lines of pale stalks to catch

Fig. 26

Fig. 27

some lights. To complete the grass effect I used a liner brush with Burnt Umber for the darker stalks and grass heads.

By repeating this procedure you can build up a section of rough grass as I have done in **fig. 27**, which features a sunlit autumn foreshore with some larks feeding. In the flatter area, texture was created by dragging a loaded Series 28 wash brush over the paper – the uneven Not surface creates a sparkle of light. The birds were not pre-planned; they were worked in after their small world had been painted. Happily they share the same colours as the grass.

In **fig. 28** I used the 'brush-dragging' technique to create a textured shape, and then with a smaller pointed brush shot into this a good strong mix of Burnt Umber and Permanent Blue to suggest the stony and lichened surface of the rock. This is an exciting process and great fun to practise. The result depends on 'happy accident'. I broke the rules, in fact, by painting a pale wash of blue-grey over the contrasting areas of colour (by then dry) to suggest modelling in the rock and the emergent ptarmigan. I used a warm Yellow Ochre to surround the rock with grass and to begin working into the bird's plumage.

Fig. 28

Portraying feathers

Feathers are as beautiful in the mass as they are individually. **Fig. 29** features some brush exercises which show how to build up feather masses. Try practising these, and then expand on them with some of your own variations.

In the two examples of black plumage (**a, b**), note how they reflect a surprising amount of light. The top example, which might represent a coot's plumage, is matt black. I mixed a wash of Burnt Umber and Permanent Blue to achieve this, adding a deeper colour at the bottom to suggest roundness and shade. Over this I used a fine brush to paint lines in an even darker tone to lift a feather here and there. The lower example, a raven's or crow's plumage, painted with a Dalon Series D77 brush, is far glossier. The general rule is that feathers appear lighter on the upper parts of the bird. However, the barb structure results in the upper half of each individual feather often appearing slightly darker.

For the female mallard's flank feathers (**c**) I underpainted with Yellow Ochre, using the same brush as before, carefully masking out the pale edges and marks on each feather. Over this I painted a Burnt Umber, darkening the upper halves of the feathers, but lightening the whole group towards the top.

The top sequence of examples (**d**) starts with some brush strokes representing loose breast feathers, of an owl perhaps. While these were still wet, I used a fine brush to introduce a Burnt Umber for the streak down the middle of each feather. I added ox-gall solution to this last colour so that it did not spread too much. Next I overpainted with a blue wash to indicate shadow and then added a fine line on each feather for the quill. Lastly I overpainted masking fluid on some of the feathers and washed in more tone to lift the feathers a little. I then added fine barring to each feather.

The middle sequence (**e**) illustrates a pheasant's wing coverts. These were painted in Burnt Sienna using a square-tipped brush. I added the individual black edgings later with a Series D66 No. 7 brush. If these are painted over a tonally graduated blue wash, the light, shade and contour are reinforced.

The lower examples (**f**) show three graduated colour washes: the first from the left suggests downy plumage; the second has a scaly quality because the masked-out edges of the feathers are light; the third is of fine black-edged feathering descending and overlapping like tiles.

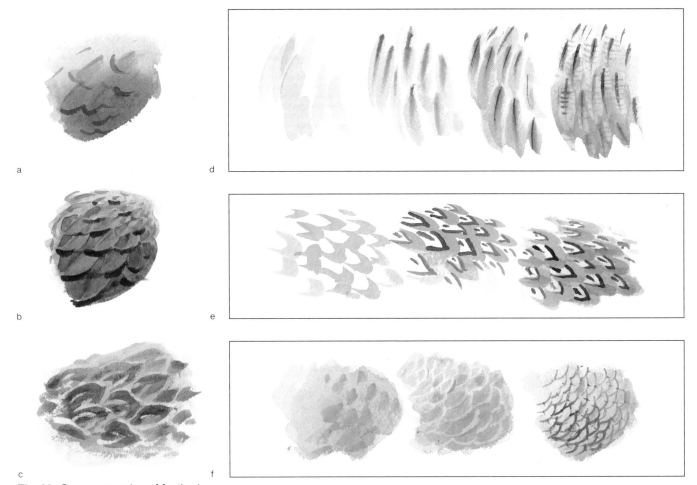

a

b

c

d

e

f

Fig. 29 Some examples of feathering

Fig. 30

Fig. 31

Fig. 32

BIRD SHAPE AND FORM

Birds, of course, develop from the egg, and they retain something of that compact and satisfying shape all their lives, from chick to adult. In the smaller birds this is very obvious. In others the shape may be elongated or disguised with a long tail or neck, or broad wings. But however different the bird, or however complex in pattern and variety the plumage may be, you will find that it is always helpful to visualize this shape underlying its form when you study a bird.

All of us have probably doodled the egg/bird shape at least once in our lives. Try it now more seriously with a liner brush, fully charged with watercolour (**fig. 30**). The egg shape has an underlying rhythm; try to catch it. The springiness of the brush will help. Work freely from the wrist. Practise the shape, then add another smaller egg, slightly overlapping the first, for the head. Find the eye and bill with a horizontal stroke to produce a thrush shape. Find the tail with a line from the eye through to the base of the egg. **Fig. 31** illustrates a bullfinch seen from the front and from the side. Note how its shape is more elongated and how from the front the head overlaps the body.

Have fun lengthening or shaping the bill, enlarging the eye or the head, shortening or lengthening the wings, tail and legs. The combinations are endless (**fig. 32**). Put yourself in charge of evolution; create new species. One thing you can be sure of: no matter how eccentric your bird, it is already alive and flourishing somewhere in the world!

A bird's shape will express its feelings. This means that with accurate observation you can portray these and establish the mood of a composition. For example, a bird with its head up is stretched alert to danger, creating a mood of anxiety and expectation. A sleeping bird, however, is relaxed and round, its plumage fluffed up. As you watch and draw from living birds you will become aware of just how changeable their shape is.

Let's now look at how birds manage such radical changes of shape. The first clue is in their bone structure. Look at the diagram I have painted (**fig. 33**). You will see that the back to front 'knee' is not a knee at all; it's an ankle. The true knee is higher up the leg, close to the body and hidden under plumage. This means that the 'leg' that is obvious to us is really an extended foot. The bird is therefore constantly 'on its toes', which must account for some of its agility. Try the pose yourself: crouch down with your knees up to your chest and balance on your toes. In birds the arrangement of their bones allows them to crouch low and to stretch up with equal facility.

The bones forming the body are fixed together and modified to take the bulk of powerful flight muscles. These are bedded and wrapped along the sternum to form the breast. The wings themselves, when at rest, lie along the body and their bones resemble the bones of a human arm, with the wrist and hand, from which spring the main flight feathers, held back and down. I describe more fully the way in which a bird extends its wings in the section on birds in flight (see page 32).

Apart from the wings, there is one other part of a bird which dramatically changes its shape, and that is its neck. Look at these mallards resting and on the alert (**fig. 34**). It is of course the neck that makes the difference here.

The long-necked giraffe has seven vertebrae in its neck, but the house sparrow, tiny as it is, has fourteen! These are connected more tenuously than in humans and the head swivels on one pivot not two. Thus the heads and necks of all birds have enormous freedom of movement and flexibility, which accounts for the owl's ability to move its head through 180° while its body remains still. Other birds can do this, too – when they roost, for example – but normally have no need to as their eyes are placed on the sides of their heads, giving them all-round vision.

So, because of their flexible structure, we must expect birds, as we study them, to assume all manner of serpentine and elastic poses, and to be capable of extreme contraction or elongation. By visualizing the bone structure beneath these contortions, you will be able to grasp what is going on.

Let's look at the other factors that affect shape. To help here I have done a brush drawing of a blackbird, showing the main feather masses and their names (**fig. 35**). Over the crown, under the chin and the ear coverts the feathers are small and close-fitting, visually indistinguishable from each other. They become progressively larger and longer towards the wing tips and tail. Individual feathers are laid over each other like roof slates so that they resist wind, rain and dust. When the bird is preening with individual feathers ruffled there are fine shadows under the lower edge of each one.

Usually the feathers fall into recognizable masses, which simplify study considerably. The ear coverts are a useful guide to dividing the head proportions into crown, chin and nape, and they indicate where the neck feathers start even when the bird is at rest. The folded wing fits under the wing coverts, the primaries and secondaries slotting away under each other like a Chinese fan. Likewise the tail feathers, when not in use, are stowed away under the middle and longest one. The flank feathers form a mass and can be expanded, flattened or raised over the wing area to meet the wing coverts. You see this happening especially in cold weather,

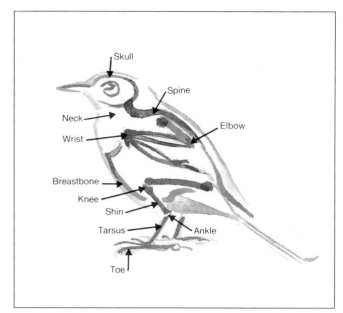

Fig. 33

Fig. 34

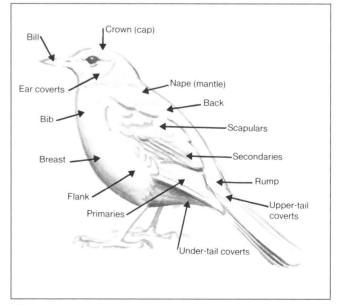

Fig. 35

Fig. 36

Fig. 37

Fig. 38

as shown by the fieldfare in **fig. 36** (top left) keeping warm. In the same illustration other birds demonstrate various body shapes.

Each feather has its own muscle, and each feather mass can be raised or lowered independently for preening, sunning, display or excitement. This is often strikingly illustrated when birds are dust-bathing.

Feathers are an outer skin moulded over an elastic and flexible structure. Walking, hopping or flying, birds express this fluidity with intrinsic rhythms that are their own. These studies of Canada geese resting, feeding and walking suggest the rhythms peculiar to them (**fig. 37**).

The rhythmic walk of a long-legged bird like the avocet is different. In **fig. 38** I have drawn an avocet in a number of poses demonstrating various leg positions and how they work together. To step forward the bird must lift its ankle quite high (from the rear the legs may appear to cross over), especially in mud or water. This means its stride is long and elegant.

Different head shapes

Fig. 39 features some studies of the heads of water birds, which show variations on a theme, and some owls, which are markedly different in shape. At the top are the heads of a male (left) and female (right) eider. This is a hardy sea-going duck and its sturdiness is expressed in the strong wedge-shape of its head. The sharp division into black and white areas in the male does not appear to correspond to the fall of the feathers; it cuts across the head and hides the eye.

The next duck, a pochard, is a handsome bird with a higher and more rounded forehead than the eider. From the front the features fit into an oval format. It takes consistent drawing practice to master the shape of a duck's bill when foreshortened, as here. Just how different front and side views may look is demonstrated by the great crested grebe, below the pochard. From the side the heron-like head of this bird expands out to the 'tippet' and crest (which can be raised at will), and from the front this summer decoration can create a circular shape divided by the thin black triangle of the crown.

Beneath the grebe are two sea-birds whose characters seem totally opposed. The herring gull has a low brow with a glittering yellow eye, axe-like bill and a turned-down mouth, giving it a cruel and ruthless look. The puffin, in contrast, reminds one of a clown, even down to its eye 'make-up' and multi-coloured bill. Analysing these expressions is of great help in capturing the character of a bird's head. Note how the puffin's bill is really quite a simple shape, even when foreshortened as it is here. The head divides into easily explained shapes when seen simply as black with white leaf-shaped side panels.

Finally, we come to the owls: a long-eared owl, tawny owl (side and front view), and a little owl with its stern 'eyebrows' and fierce yellow eyes. As a family, owls seem able to effect radical changes of shape from minute to minute. Their enormous heads consist mainly of feathers and these can be puffed up or slimmed down. The long-eared owl's ears are, of course, not ears at all but feathery crests which can be raised or lowered. They are a draughtsman's delight. The heads themselves present big, sculptural shapes, while the discs around the eyes provide big and defined areas offering scope for rhythm of line.

Portraying birds' feet

Perching birds have feet which possess a hind claw for extra grip on twigs and branches (**fig. 40**). On the ground most of these birds hop to overcome the trailing toe. When stationary the bird spreads its foot to form a 'stand': the rear and front toes are in alignment, while the other toes splay out on each side from the tarsus. Each toe has two joints like the human finger and is thus very flexible.

The simplest means of visualizing how the feet grip a twig is to see the clenched foot as a 'fist' such as made by the human hand, with the rear toe and claw hanging down behind. If the toes are splayed over a large branch they spread into a variety of positions as required. This flexibility offers multiple gripping positions on, for instance, a vertical branch.

Some diving birds, like cormorants, have webbed feet, but these are still capable of gripping and perching. When drawing these, you will find the line of the web provides a useful means of defining the position of the toes.

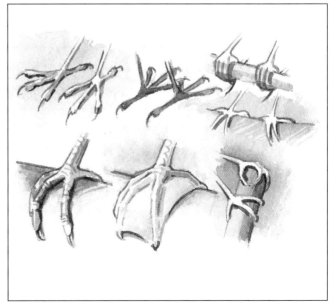

Fig. 39 Different head shapes

Fig. 40 Birds' feet

Establishing a bird's character

Walking birds We are all aware that a long neck, shovel bill, boat-like body and paddle feet add up to 'duck' (**fig. 42**). We know as well that its shape is largely determined by its aquatic way of life. But what, I wonder, determined the shelduck's plumage? It could serve as a demonstration lecture on feather masses, being as they are conveniently and sharply defined by contrasting colours. The bird also possesses a chestnut brown halter around its breast, which is of great help when it comes to understanding its contours, even when the bird is asleep and appears to be little more than a 'shapeless' mass. When standing, its 'golf club' head, full breast and sloping stance offer a strong and rhythmic shape.

The single most important feature of a pheasant must be the length of its tail (**fig. 43**). When the bird is feeding this is held downwards or horizontally; when up and running, the tail is cocked at an angle. It is this kind of information that enables you to establish the balance and pose of the bird rapidly, even when it is moving. Notice the foreshortening that takes place when the tail is pointing towards you, as in the hen on the left.

All the game birds have a satisfying sculptural and compact form, often raising their upper-tail coverts in cold weather, which creates chunky and distinctive shapes. If their crop (in their lower neck) is crammed with grain, like in the cock pheasant in the middle, it can add a sense of weight to balance out the tail feathers.

For these pheasants I picked out their shapes with simple washes of Burnt Umber and Crimson Alizarin. Colourwise, these birds tend to blend with foliage, especially in autumn. This is in contrast to the shelduck, whose plumage allows it to be picked out on an estuary even at great distances.

Fig. 44 illustrates the round and compact shapes of three snipe: one alert, one feeding, and one resting. Their feathers are streaked and mottled, and take some study to grasp; but once understood, they are of great assistance in suggesting direction and contours. The distinctive feature of this bird's shape must always be the bill, which is like an extension of its head. It forms a powerful directional line, which is something to take account of in composition. When the bird is at rest. there is an 'S'-shaped feeling about it, as it coils its neck and balances its bill on its breast. Note how when these birds turn towards us their shape becomes more circular.

The colours I used for this painting consist of a wash of Yellow Ochre, overpainted with mixtures of Burnt Sienna, Burnt Umber and Permanent Blue. The dead grasses in the background were stroked in with a liner brush using Burnt Sienna.

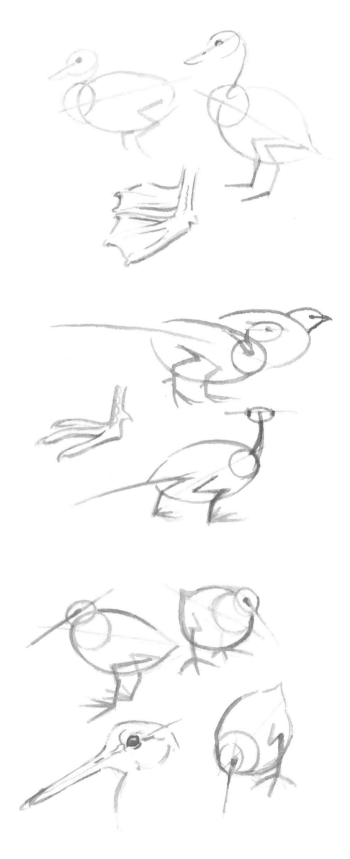

Fig. 41 Studies based on the paintings opposite

28

Fig. 42 (*top*) Shelduck, **fig. 43** (*centre*) Pheasant and **fig. 44** (*bottom*) Snipe

Perching birds In contrast to those on the preceding pages all these birds possess a long hind claw for gripping and perching. The kestrel is one of Britain's best-known birds of prey; here I have done three studies of it (**fig. 46**). The first bird is upright and relaxed, possibly digesting a meal. The second one, grasping the wire, is balancing against the breeze, scanning the ground for prey. The third has just alighted and is poised to take off again.

From the front the falcon's head, with its large dark forward-facing eyes and wide gape, presents a decidedly frog-like aspect. The head itself is flat-crowned and is squarish both from the front and side. These birds make fine subjects for drawing as their feather masses divide themselves into neat and contoured shapes. Their feet are used for capturing prey and look disproportionally large. In flight falcons are slim and streamlined; at rest they can double their bulk by relaxing their feathers.

Magpies are intelligent and cheeky birds. I admire their 'wicked' innocence and any portrait of them should try to capture this quality (**fig. 47**). Their plumage is a designer's delight. The feather masses overlap clearly in alternate black and white sections. This means that however contorted the shapes of the bird become, while preening or playing the acrobat, they are easy to understand. This is further assisted by the dynamic line of the long tail, which assumes all directions in a high wind or when the bird is simply balancing itself.

The body is, of course, 'pied'; the black head, cape, and breast are contrasted with white on the belly, flanks and wing coverts. The primaries return to black and merge with the tail coverts and the tail itself. A blue sheen is refracted off the wings and various greens off the tail. From the front the head shape is squarish, but from the side it is rounder, merging into the powerful corvine bill. The bird will stand out clearly in any landscape. My favourite background is blackthorn blossom, which echoes the bird's colour.

The missel is a large elegant thrush with a loud rattling call (**fig. 48**). It is bold and aggressive, famed for its spirited defence of its nest against birds such as magpies. Its plumage is spotted more boldly than that of the song thrush and all its wing feathers are picked out with pale edges.

Every bird has its own facial expression. The missel thrush has large dark eyes and raised 'eyebrows' which give it a naïve expression. This is an illusion, of course, but it is clues like this that can give us an idea as to whether our portrait is conveying the bird's appearance correctly.

The thrush in the middle is rounder than the other two because it is colder; as a result its flank feathers are fluffed around its body and the head is tucked back into its nape.

Fig. 45 Studies based on the paintings opposite

Fig. 46 (*top*) Kestrel, **fig. 47** (*centre*) Magpie and **fig. 48** (*bottom*) Missel thrush

BIRDS IN FLIGHT

Portraying flight is the great challenge to the bird painter. From the soaring grace of the eagle to the fluttering of the goldfinch, the flight patterns of birds present complexities of shape, movement and speed that can baffle the beginner – and, indeed, the experienced painter.

Happily there is a wealth of photography from which to study flight action in birds, and by drawing and painting from photographs you can begin to understand the way that wings work and the perspectives involved. On the other hand, however, nothing is more static than a flying bird frozen by the camera. The flow and interaction of bird, wing, air and space are banished by the precise speed of the shutter. A quick brush sketch which is an instinctive response to movement and rhythm is often more 'truthful' than a pedantic representation of every flight feather.

The little sketch in **fig. 49**, for example, successfully summons up the fluttering touch-down of a duck. Obviously the bird itself doesn't pass muster, for the purpose of the sketch is to suggest flow, mobility and movement. This sense of movement depends to an extent on a 'natural' distortion, that which re-creates the blur, the mixture of shapes, which our eyes are too slow to perceive individually. In fact, the blur is all we see in the flight of smaller birds, which can hardly be expressed otherwise.

The flat, square-tipped brushes, like the Daler-Rowney Series 55 or Dalon Series D88 in their various sizes, are extremely useful for sketches like the ones on these pages. This is because their calligraphic qualities of thick and thin strokes can solve some of the perspective problems presented by outstretched wings in a single movement (or two!).

Capturing the 'jizz' or character of a bird

Let's start with that simplest evocation of flight, the time-honoured cliché used by all children for the seagull, as illustrated in **fig. 50a**. As a shape it's not at all bad; it has a sense of direction, movement and buoy-

Fig. 50

ancy. With the assistance of the calligraphic properties of your brush, however, you can immediately give the shape a sense of space and perspective (**fig. 50b**). By experimenting further with the thick/thin zigzag strokes that the brush produces, you can suggest the angled wings of the gull (**fig. 50c**). By altering these angles you can imply leisurely or urgent flight; by extending the wing span, body size or tail length you can conjure up a variety of bird types.

Already you can see how brushwork alone is able to summon up the character or 'jizz' of the bird's flight, that combination of factors that enables the bird-watcher almost by instinct to recognize a bird at a distance. In **fig. 51**, for instance, the flight of a buzzard can be suggested by inverting the stroke, drawing the brush from right to left with a rising stroke, which gives it a floating quality. This device might be useful for landscape painters who want to give life to their skies and suggest aerial perspectives. In exactly the same way a bevy of rooks, perhaps, tumbling in the wind, could be rendered by multi-directional flicks of the brush.

Fig. 49

Fig. 51

Fig. 52

Fig. 53

Fig. 54

Fig. 55

Fig. 56

The heron is a stately, rather lumbering flier, its mastery of the air revealed when it descends dramatically from on high to its tree-top nest. Its wings are broad, and in flight its legs trail and its neck is tucked back into its shoulder. In **fig. 52** I created the bird by doubling the downstroke on the wings with the square-tipped brush and using a side stroke, with its thin edge, for the trailing legs and suggestion of head and beak. I touched in the upturned primaries on the near wing; they are, of course, equally upturned on the far wing – but invisible to us from this angle.

Birds of the woodland, like the sparrowhawk, blackbird and pheasant, have roundish wings and long tails. They are designed for explosive acceleration and manoeuvrability through close trees. To work out the pheasant's wing shape in **fig. 53** I used my brush in a circular motion, leading off to the right with side strokes for the long primary feathers. Pheasants fly with their heads up, in contrast to birds of prey which peer down or ahead. It is details like this that determine the 'jizz' of the bird.

For the other three bird shapes here I worked from photographs, relying on speed and dexterity of brushwork to give the birds the liveliness of active flight. Notice how the gliding sea-birds are very different in shape from the pheasant; they have long wings and slender bodies. They don't need the large breast muscles that give the pheasant its barrel shape. In its travels the gannet (**fig. 54**) will spend a lot of time skimming the waves with its wings held flat or decurved. The wings can appear double-jointed because the bird folds them back to plunge into the sea after fish. The skua shape was achieved by holding the brush at a flat angle and working more horizontally (**fig. 55**). Lastly, **fig. 56** shows a flying swan, its neck curved in rhythm with its wing beat. The momentum is all in the head and neck, striving forward, in contrast to a pheasant, say, where the tail appears to trail behind.

You will notice that in all these sketches I've treated the wing as a single blade or aerofoil. More detailed studies of the wings require a little more knowledge of the main feather shapes and the dynamics of flight itself.

The way birds fly

The dynamics of bird flight are complex, but logical. All bird artists should know something about the mechanisms of feathers which enable birds to fly, but at the same time it is important not to concentrate on detail at the expense of a sense of the 'feel' and 'rhythm' of the flying bird.

If you examine your arm, from fingertips to shoulder, you will see that it has affinities to the wing and wing-bone structure of a bird (see **fig. 57**). If you spread your fingers to represent the bird's 'hand' with its primary feathers and your thumb to represent the alula or 'winglet' (used by the bird to assist in low-speed flight), if you bend back your hand at the wrist, as does the bird, hold your elbows in and your forearms forward, you can almost imagine you are flying and feel the breeze as the air whistles past you.

Now, if you raise your 'wings' and contract them as the female duck at the rear is doing in **fig. 58**, the air will be allowed in through the feathers and around the wings. On the downbeat the wings straighten up and thrust down, while the primaries, secondaries and tertiaries extend and press together as one to compress the gathered air and push upon it, as the drake mallard is doing. This, as you can see, forces the bird upwards into the air. The dabbling ducks, like the mallard, are renowned for their explosive take-offs. Their deep-breasted appearance is formed by the large flight muscles that power this action.

The wing movements of the gliding birds with longer, narrower wings are similar to the mallard's but less extreme. By bringing the wings closer to the body, wind resistance is lessened and the bird's speed increases. By spreading them wide, it will gain lift and rise. Changes of direction are effected by banking, or contracting one wing, to decrease drag on one side, as well as by fanning out the tail. The bird involves its whole body in the act of flying.

Look at the main masses of the feathers in **fig. 58** and see how they fold over each other and fan out. The longest feathers are at the tip of the wing and spread out like the fingers of a hand. The secondaries and wing coverts above and below pad out the wing surface to form an aerofoil section. It helps to see the wing as a single shape made up of these principal shapes, formed by these masses. Once you see these clearly, the detail of the feathers can be more easily placed. Note that the feathers get smaller nearer the front edge.

Opposite, I have painted a group of mallards descending, in contrast to those in **fig. 58**. I derived the shapes from photographic evidence, my sketchbooks and my own 'feel' for flight. The birds are half-gliding, half-parachuting down. All the while they are spilling

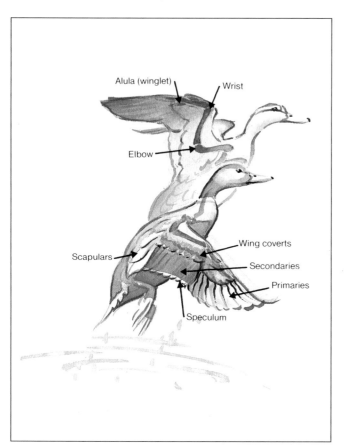

Fig. 57 Mallards: feather and bone structure in flight

Fig. 58 Mallards taking off

Fig. 59 Mallards
descending

h

g

Fig. 60 Black-headed gull circling

air from their wings, with their heads up to watch their descent. The birds at the bottom would be beating their wings rapidly to reduce speed and impact as they lower their undercarriages and spread their tails in order to alight. A stretch of water would allow them a longer 'sea-plane' approach, but here landing space is confined and the descent is therefore more dramatic. In this painting the birds are both above and below eye-level, which helps to emphasize the cascading effect.

A bird on the wing

There are a few devices I have found useful when sketching birds in flight. First, as I have said before, treat the body, wings and tail as one – go for the rhythm of flight. Put down just a few squiggles if you like, as you watch; and with groups of birds, look for the larger shapes formed by the group rather than the individual birds. You'll find you can add detail to them later.

Second, try 'snapshot' memorizing. Imagine your eye is the shutter of a camera. As the bird moves across your field of vision, focus on it and shut your eyes. The image is for a brief instant photographed on your ret-ina; it is isolated, 'frozen' long enough for you to draw it. With practice you can improve your memory skills considerably in this way.

The black-headed gull illustrated in **fig. 60** is in winter plumage. It is found as commonly in town parks as in fields and on estuaries, and is easily tempted to approach by the prospect of food.

Imagine this bird is circling in front of you, intent on a bag of crusts in your hand. Take up your sketchbook and pencil and let the bird enchant you with its delicacy and grace as it flies towards you. Already our gull

a

b

f

e

is eyeing the paper bag. As it approaches, the head and body are condensed into one and the wings are slender suggestions of their true shape, consisting mainly of their leading edge. The bird turns to pass us and keels away gently. At this point the body is beginning to resemble its true profile (**a**). The wings have bent slightly and we can glimpse a portion of the underwing on both sides as the bird tilts. Note the offside wing is leading.

The gull's flight, at present, is relaxed and gliding. It is now almost ahead of us, and although the offside wing is still leading it is more hidden by the head (**b**). It turns to begin another cycle and the offside wing moves behind the body. Now the nearside wing is dramatically foreshortened, condensed into a thin shape. We glimpse the bird's red feet and legs and, end on, the tail, closed for gliding flight (**c**).

The gull now turns again and flaps more deeply for a new and tighter circle. Its shape begins to resemble that of its original approach. Note how the bird is half looking back (**d**). As it circles around, the nearside wing is forward and conceals the head (**e**). On the upbeat we would see the body and head. The bird continues the circle and on the downbeats we can see the pattern on its upper wing, which is foreshortened with a slight lift of the primaries (**f**). The gull is now gliding lazily with its wings hanging down (**g**). The far wing is beginning to overtake as it turns again towards us, although we can't actually see much of it except the wrist.

The bird then flaps a little to pick up speed (**h**). The near wing presents a thin edge while the other gives a view of the upper surface. The head becomes more prominent. The gull then gradually turns towards us and begins to assume its original shape (**a**).

c

d

USING A SKETCHBOOK

A sketchbook should become your indispensable companion. It can offer you invaluable opportunities to develop your powers of observation, your instant drawing skills, and your brain's astonishing capacity for memory. I have completed about ten now in as many years and I enjoy leafing back through them as the pages conjure up many happy memories.

As a sketchbook is not meant for other eyes it can be as rough and untidy as you like; for this reason, sketchbooks can often have great charm. The drawings in them are authentic and timely, done for yourself without self-consciousness; that is what makes them good.

Your sketchbook will be rained on, snowed on, and coffee-stained if it goes everywhere with you – as it should do. You should never worry about whether the drawings look good or not; I have based many paintings on sketches which are quite indecipherable to others. Yet these little drawings often carry home those nuggets of information that have inspired me at the time.

There are times when you are able to draw continuously. I have spent many happy hours sketching in a public park, sitting in a deck-chair and surrounded by ducks, geese, swans and other birds. Zoos and hides on nature reserves are excellent places for drawing as well.

Always remember that drawing is the result of close observation, so draw only after you have observed and only when you are ready to. At times, a sequence or series of events in bird behaviour demands particular observation and understanding before you can put pencil to paper. Here it is the quality of looking that counts, so take your time. How well you observe depends on your enjoyment and appreciation of the wealth of beauty before your eyes. While you watch a duck preening, sparrows dust-bathing or a blackbird sunbathing, you can at the same time visualize to yourself the lines you would draw to define the shape and main directions of the pose. As you gain confidence in your powers of observation you can also make mental notes of the colours and shadows which suggest light.

When the movements of the birds are too rapid and you catch only a quick glimpse of a warbler or thrush in the hedgerow a rough squiggle is often all you can get down. Indeed, a hasty squiggle can convey much more than you might think. You can fill in more details later, although if you are quiet and relaxed the bird will often reappear in its bush. I sometimes work on the sketches further when I get home while the day's events are still fresh in my mind's eye.

When the weather is good and you have planned a less hectic day, take a watercolour block out with you. This is ideal for making notes on landscape, and with your watercolour box to call on there is very little that cannot be simplified and put down quickly and accurately. You will need a stool as well, and you may decide to take an easel. I usually choose a habitat like a riverbank or boggy field (into which I can later incorporate a suitable bird, like a moorhen or heron), or a subject such as brambles, perhaps, between which a wren might slip.

You should always be aware of the surrounding countryside as you sketch birds; it is worth making a conscious effort to stop and record it, as you never know when these sketches might provide useful reference for the background of one of your paintings. I

Fig. 61 House martins and sand martins

Fig. 62 Great crested grebes

often sketch corners of the countryside that catch my eye, or details of leaves and undergrowth, or perhaps an old wrought iron gate that might be just the thing on which to sit any one of a number of hedgerow birds at a later point (**fig. 63**). This is the type of subject matter that is discovered only by the observant eye and it can be of immense value. Take care to note all the details, such as the nuts and bolts of the gate, and the old nail hammered into the gatepost for no apparent reason. Observations of this sort add to the authenticity of your background.

Using binoculars while sketching simultaneously can leave the biceps feeling like aching strings and seems to require more hands than evolution has given us! Pace yourself; take a good long look through the glasses, and then draw. If you are settled down comfortably you can use what is known as a bino-support, a harness arrangement that supports the binoculars before your eyes while you sketch.

Although there can be no substitute for direct observation, I find my camera invaluable for recording back-up detail and habitats. My telephoto lens (70–210 mm) helps to frame up a few brambles, for example, or can take in wider views of a field or pool perhaps. Luckily this lens is not powerful enough to photograph birds unless they are very near, so I am not faced with agonizing decisions as to whether to peer through the lens or pick up my sketchbook.

I always sketch in conjunction with the camera; I draw first to capture the feel of the place and then often record the detail with the camera. Remember that a camera cannot capture the perspective of our binocular vision, and only rarely does it suggest the sensations we experience when confronted with the colour and movement of nature. As I mentioned earlier, I use colour prints rather than transparencies and I now have an enormous reference collection of snow scenes, woodland pictures, and seascapes, etc. All these are extremely helpful when composing paintings.

As time goes on and you look back through your sketchbooks you will be amazed at the truth and liveliness that your little sketches and notes convey. It may seem impossible to re-create these qualities in larger compositions – a truth with which Rembrandt and Constable were only too familiar – but the value of sketches is that you can return to them again and again for authentic information. Yes, you did see a song thrush next to a snipe in a meadow; yes, the heron was that shape when it landed on its nest. I still return to my earliest sketchbook if it has recorded the grebe or warbler that I now need for my composition.

As you practise your sketches you will improve. You will also discover what really interests you and how to capture it on paper quickly and effectively. As you combine all the approaches mentioned here you will build up a stock of information so that your sketchbook will

Fig. 63 Reference sketch for background material

become a sourcebook of inspiration as you tackle larger paintings.

One last hint: put your name and address on the inside cover of your sketchbook. The dreaded time may arrive when you get home to find your precious book has escaped from your anorak pocket; a year's hard work lost – but regained when some kindly birdwatcher or shepherd posts it back.

Finding new sketching opportunities

If perhaps you find it difficult to get out to the countryside or local park to sketch, there are nevertheless other options available to you. For a start you can look out of your window and watch the birds in your garden or street. **Fig. 64** (overleaf) shows some sketches I made from my window. As I watched, a young starling appeared, newly fledged, by the French windows. Its stumpy tail and large feet almost turn it into a caricature. Two wood pigeons visited, when they thought things were quiet, and collected twigs for their untidy nest. Lastly, a jay appeared – an exotic-looking visitor with a parrot-like screech. Its patchwork-coloured plumage presents a real challenge to the artist.

Fig. 64 Sketches made from the artist's window

Alternatively you can watch television! The quality of nature films is now so high that for artists they are almost as good as the real thing. The guillemots in **fig. 65** were filmed swimming (or flying) under water in pursuit of their food – sand eels. This provided an unrivalled opportunity to study form and function and experience the secret life of water birds. I made a note on my sketches of their 'silvery' colour so that I would remember to use this colour theme in my composition. The puffin and tern also appeared in the same documentary.

Fig. 66 also features some drawings done rapidly from another wonderful film on television about the life of the golden eagle. Often shots of a bird in flight are shown in slow motion which enables you to study wing forms as the bird plays with the air currents or swoops in on its prey. Notice the huge beak of the eagle and its forward-facing eyes. Also scattered over the page of my sketchbook (hoping not to be noticed!) are sketches of the bird's prey – the mountain hare and the ptarmigan.

You may be lucky enough to know an enthusiast who keeps birds. The falconer who keeps the birds illustrated in **fig. 67** regularly hires them out as models. I worked hard and continuously as I sketched this active barn owl and impressive buzzard, leaving a pose if necessary when one of the birds moved and returning to it later. As a result some of the sketches are rough. I added colour in places later.

Fig. 65 Sketches of sea-birds made from television

Fig. 66 Studies of a golden eagle made from television

Fig. 67 Barn owls and buzzards

BIRD PORTRAIT 1
THE LAPWING

Every bird artist has a favourite subject to which he or she frequently returns. Mine must be the lapwing, so named because of its wing shape. Country folk refer to it as the peewit after its call.

The lapwing has everything: a thrilling aerobatic display over its spring meadow; spectacular flocks that switch from black to white as they wheel over the winter furrows; a jaunty cockade; and not least a dark plumage shot through with gorgeous optical colours. The bird is common in fields and easy to watch.

I've chosen the lapwing to paint in depth because its plumage is iridescent. This is a well-known characteristic and is seen on the plumage of birds as diverse as the kingfisher, the peacock, the farmyard cockerel, and even the suburban starling. Usually the colours of iridescence are blue to green, but from other directions the same feathers can appear purple or crimson. It is this contradictory quality that makes the phenomenon so stimulating for artists.

The shimmering colours are the result of light waves glancing off microscopic but regular dark granules in the feather barbs. Without incident light – that is, light falling across a surface – the feathers look grey or black, which in essence they are.

First stage I approached the painting of the lapwing exactly as I always do, checking reference photographs and noting the sloping bill, the large eye, and the pink colour of the leg. I decided to use Saunders Waterford 140 lb (300 gsm) Not paper.

I began with the crest, using a flick of the liner brush, loaded with a pale mix of Permanent Blue and Burnt Umber, to establish rhythm. I drew the brush down and round the breast and belly, and then marked out the features – the eye, the crown, the bib. Next I put in the shadow on the belly and under-tail coverts.

Second stage I suggested some reflected warmth on the breast with a mix of pale Yellow Ochre and a hint of Cadmium Red, and painted in the orange under-tail coverts with Indian Red. Next I tackled the iridescent back. With the lapwing, instead of the feather masses lightening towards the upper parts, as they do on a partridge, for instance, they darken. The nearest analogy I

Fig. 68 First stage

Fig. 69 Second stage

can suggest for the lapwing is a green glass bottle through which coloured light passes but which darkens at the sides where the light cannot pass through the 'thicker' glass. Thus you will notice that I have deepened the shadow not only under the wing but also on the upper edge of the bird, the upper edges of each feather group, the wrist of the wing, the scapulars and the mantle. To an extent, therefore, the general rule of shading is reversed.

I then washed in pale yellow-green on the wings, leaving a space to feed in Crimson Alizarin on the wing coverts, and worked in Permanent Blue over the wing joint. The bib is not markedly iridescent so I painted it dark blue/brown, using French Ultramarine and Burnt Umber, allowing the colour to merge into the nape while wet. I used the same colour for strengthening the face markings – the cap, crest and eyes.

Finished stage The lapwing's legs are pink-red and I put these in next with a line of shadow down one side and with body shadow on the leg furthest away. I then strengthened all the colours in the painting and put in the shadows under individual feathers. Finally I painted in the shadow on the ground.

Small amounts of the same colours used for the bird were brushed in to build up the background of young wheat. I wanted to depict warmth and sunlight, so the colour of the earth reflected this.

Fig. 71 Group of lapwings showing how their varied angles produce different colours

Fig. 70 Finished stage

43

BIRD PORTRAIT 2
THE GREY HERON

Anyone who lives near a river or lake will know the heron well – a large bird with a slow lumbering flight. While fishing, it can stand without moving for long periods and in a variety of attitudes.

It is one of those birds which can change its shape dramatically. It can stretch out to pencil slimness, or bunch itself into a sculptural and compact mass. I have seen herons in so many different poses that it is impossible for any single one to sum up the bird completely.

In colour it is a satisfying blueish grey, which lightens towards its back and mantle. Its head is well marked, with a swept-back 'eyebrow' which is useful for defining its eye position and head shape. It can raise this crest when displaying. Its breast is streaked with long plumes in black, which again help to define the shape. Its wings fold and close over its back, like those of a beetle.

If your intention is to paint a relaxed, even restful picture, then a pose where the heron is practically asleep while digesting a full crop of fish would be the one to choose. A fishing heron, however, would suggest alertness and purpose. The whole tenor of your painting would be quite different if you decided to use this pose.

Before I started the painting in this exercise I looked through my sketchbooks to see what sketches of herons I had. The one in **fig. 72** struck me as interesting.

I then practised some free brushwork drawings capturing the broken 'S' rhythm of the heron's neck (**fig. 73**). This underlying rhythm is often present in other birds with long necks, too, and it is helpful to bear it in mind when you are drawing them. In the heron it is caused by the special 'snap' mechanism that enables the bird to flick its head forward instantaneously to spear fish.

I also decided to practise drawing some details of the head and feathers (**fig. 74**). I concentrated particularly on the position of the eye in relation to the bill, and the way the chin is extended along and under the lower mandible. I also rehearsed the 'eyebrow' stripe and crest, and the overall shape and poise of the head and neck.

The position I finally chose for the bird in my painting was the resting one – a pose I had noticed a while back on one of my expeditions. The heron was resting on saltings in an estuary and was perhaps digesting a meal or waiting for the tide to come in. There was powerful sunlight on the bird and it was clearly lit up against the dark mud bank with lots of reflected light in its subtle grey plumage. It was still sitting there twenty minutes later when I had drawn it and gave me plenty of time to look again at my sketch and correct it where necessary. This enabled me to retain a keen image of the bird in my memory.

Fig. 72

Fig. 73

Fig. 74

First stage I decided to use Saunders Waterford 140 lb (300 gsm) Not paper for the painting. I began by taking a liner brush and defining the lines of the pose in very pale blue-grey (a mixture of French Ultramarine with a touch of Burnt Umber), strengthening them when I was sure they were correct. There was a tendency here to overemphasize the bill. I tried to retain the sense of rhythm as I worked on the outline. Rhythm underlies all good drawing. It helps your grasp of the basic shape

Fig. 75 First stage

Fig. 76 Second stage

Fig. 77 Third stage

as well by encouraging you to relate the two sides of the outline as you work. Notice how the bird's legs lean back to counteract the forward impetus of the folded neck and head.

Second stage I wanted to suggest good overall illumination on the bird. This would bring out the fine warm grey of the bird's wings and back. Shadow is therefore fairly precise and limited and I strengthened this behind the folded neck and the mantle. I mixed a 'cloud' grey (Permanent Blue and Burnt Umber), which I've mentioned before, and worked it into the wings, back, and a section of the breast feathers in front of the wing joints. I also used this to plot the 'eyebrow' and position the eye.

Third stage With a pale Aureolin/Cadmium Red mixture I began to paint the bill and legs. Where the bird stands on a mud bank it spreads its toes and reveals that it possesses a hind claw.

Next I marked in the bird's charcoal grey 'shoulder' patches and under-tail coverts, in this case relaxed. I also strengthened the 'eyebrows' with this colour and allowed everything to dry thoroughly.

I then deepened the colour of the wings, leaving the back and mantle light in tone to suggest reflected illumination. I marked in the long black plumes of the

breast feathers, beginning with the shorter ones which climb over the curled neck and then using longer strokes to form the ones which pass down over the breast.

Finished stage I painted in a deeper orange down the rear of the legs to indicate shadow. I then did the same behind each toe, with a line of deep shadow underneath.

Next I hinted at the feather formation on the wing with small strokes of pale grey, and used the liner brush to sweep in the plumes on the back, which assist the suggestion of contour. I added a very pale wash of Burnt Umber, French Ultramarine and Crimson Alizarin on the breast plumes in front of the folded wings, and put in a touch of blue-grey shadow cast by the breast feathers on the cheek. Finally I added depth to the hanging plumes beneath the bird with the same blue-grey wash.

Originally I saw this bird outlined starkly against a dark mud bank. Here I have restrained the background colour in favour of an overall illumination, using a colour which echoes that of the heron – a wash of purple-grey. This was fed into the area after I had wetted it. For the muddy bank on which the heron stands I applied a deeper combination of the same purple-grey and algae-green, with blue-grey light reflections.

Fig. 78 Finished stage

BIRD PORTRAIT 3
A COVEY OF PARTRIDGE

The grey partridge is an attractive and familiar bird of the countryside and can be watched easily from a car by the roadside. In late summer family groups clan together into coveys, which provide the artist with an excellent opportunity to compose a picture around a group of birds.

In preparation for this painting I went out to make a few sketches. I parked smoothly by the roadside when I spotted the birds and watched them for some time over a low hedge. The autumn day was chilly, so they were snuggled down into their flank feathers, with their wing and tail coverts fluffed up. In contrast to their sleeker summer shape they were now almost spherical. While the flock fed and relaxed, one bird took a turn at sentry duty.

Back in the studio, when I came to paint them, I had in mind a group in which each member was turning outwards, with the furthest bird upright and alert. Having played around with various combinations I arrived at the tall triangular composition illustrated on page 51. The birds overlap each other, which has the effect of linking them as a group. If the sentry had been at the front it would have been too prominent and would have interrupted the birds in the foreground.

As in the previous exercise, before I began painting I looked through past sketches and practised some drawing and brushwork. I rehearsed the birds' shapes with the liner brush in pale blue-grey (Permanent Blue and Burnt Umber), looking for underlying rhythms and experimenting with form and shadow. The monochrome sketch here was derived from a bird which watched me from a dry-stone wall one spring morning (**fig. 79**). Its mate was hidden, presumably sitting on a nest somewhere nearby.

The head (**fig. 80**) was painted from a photograph and illustrates the bird's character, typical of the game birds – a forward emphasis to the forehead and face. Note the small shields over the nostrils. This study also shows the extent of the brick-red area over the bird's face.

In **fig. 81**, note how the circular eye is wide open and how it lifts at the top front, while the horizontal axis tilts

Fig. 80

Fig. 79

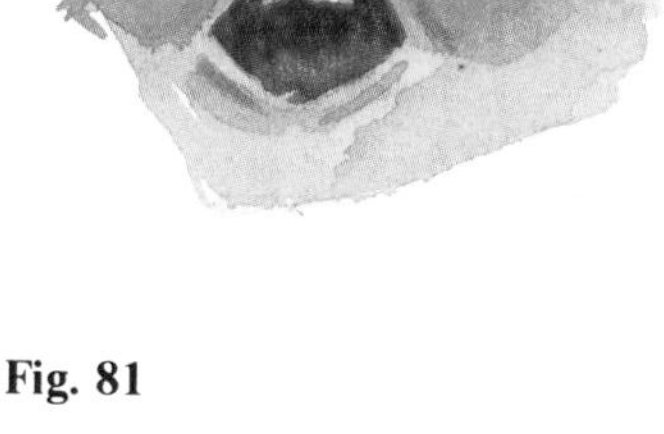

Fig. 81

Fig. 82 First stage

Fig. 83 Second stage

downwards. Again, photographic reference was useful to reacquaint me with such details. I used a pale wash of French Ultramarine for the eye, leaving a patch of white paper at the top for the highlight. When this was dry I painted in some Burnt Umber mixed with Yellow Ochre, but leaving a little of the original French Ultramarine wash untouched on each side of the highlight. When this too had dried I painted in the pupil with a dark mix of Burnt Umber and French Ultramarine, continuing this under the upper lid and the highlight. The partridge's eye is surrounded by an orbital ring, which I indicated with a line put in with a fine brush.

Plumage, of course, varies with age, sex and season, and again I went to my reference books, as well as my own notes. When it came to filling in the background later I was grateful I had put down at least a few lines on the leaves surrounding my birds as well.

I also gave some thought to the light direction, establishing it as soon as I could. A useful tip here is to make small plasticine models for this purpose and set them up under a reading light.

The partridge presents the paradox of bird painting. Its impressive stripes and mottled colours provide exciting design possibilities, but its plumage patterns are intended to disguise, camouflage, and visually disrupt its form. This is to confuse predators and artists! The solution to this problem lies in making sure your

underpainting of light and shade is well thought out and logical, so that the eye can understand and grasp the form, despite the signals the plumage gives to the contrary. This strong modelling gives you more scope to work in lighter washes over the top, without losing the sense of form.

First stage I drew in the basic shapes of the birds with the liner brush, seeking to express something of the birds' round and rhythmic outlines. I then built up the light and shade carefully with washes of pale blue-grey (Permanent Blue with a touch of Indian Red for warmth). I used Saunders Waterford 300 lb (638 gsm) Not paper, which is fairly absorbent and allows areas to be damped quickly when graduated tone is required. These washes can be blended in to produce hard and soft edges. I marked in the eyes and bills lightly, to allow correction later if necessary.

Second stage Other features were then gradually emphasized – shadows on the heads and bills, ruffled feathers, shadows under the bodies and leaves. I tried not to lose the sense of back-reflected light by overdramatizing the shading.

At this point I used a fine brush to paint in the white quills of the flank feathers with masking fluid, making sure the painting was bone-dry first.

Fig. 84 Third stage

When this monochrome stage was complete, the birds resembled nothing so much as a party of winter ptarmigan on a snow field! A careful building-up of plumage colour soon transformed the painting, however.

Third stage First I mixed the colour common to all the birds – a pale Yellow Ochre – as the base colour for the scapulars and heads. Then I added the dove grey (a mixture of Permanent Blue, Burnt Umber and Indian Red), which blends towards a yellow ochre colour on their rumps. For the broken stripes on their flank feathers I mixed a pale Burnt Umber with a hint of Crimson Alizarin. I let these stripes suggest contour; the thin square-ended brush I've already mentioned was useful here.

I wanted two of the birds to be fully plumaged males, so I mixed a bright brick red from Crimson Alizarin and Yellow Ochre and filled in the shapes of their heads. I also added a touch of the same colour to the cheeks and brows of the hens. I dotted the birds' crowns with Burnt Umber and barred the wing coverts with this colour as well.

The leaves of beet were painted with pale Sap Green mixed in a wash on damp paper to create variations, with touches of Lemon Yellow and Prussian Blue/Sap Green here and there. Streaks of Crimson Alizarin were added to indicate leaf stalks and the roots. Small touches of some of these colours were used on the soil in the foreground, over a Yellow Ochre base, for pebbles and texture. This overall colour scheme pulls the painting together.

Finished stage When all this was completed I mixed a deep Burnt Umber and French Ultramarine and put in the eyes in more detail, without forgetting the highlight in each. Slight adjustments, as always, were needed, particularly around the heads to shape them up. I sharpened up their beaks and added last ruffles to their feathers. When the painting was completely dry, I lightly rubbed out the masking fluid to reveal the fine quills on the flanks.

Fig. 85 Finished stage

GARDEN BIRDS

Field trips to the countryside can be few and far between for some of us. For all sorts of reasons we are not often as free as the birds themselves. Happily, however, gardens present plenty of opportunities for the bird artist. They can be a rich source of information and inspiration.

It depends, of course, where your home is: if it is in the country your garden will entertain a wide range of species; but even in towns it is surprising how many types of birds are attracted to a bird-table in winter. Cold weather is the time to gain the birds' confidence and their acceptance of noise and movement in the house. By moving the bird-table nearer your window, week by week, you will not even need to use binoculars to view the birds. Many of you probably feed the birds already and enjoy the daily spectacle of colour and activity outside your window. It is a good idea to keep a sketchbook and pencil near at hand on the windowsill.

The common birds can be all too easily dismissed. After all, when was the last time you actually looked closely at a house sparrow (**figs. 86** and **87**)? Personally, I find the bird fascinating and have drawn and painted sparrows over the years with great interest. A sparrow has a perky vitality, often expressed through its quarrelsome nature. Its black 'burglar' mask gives the male bird a perpetually bad-tempered expression, but this is unfair of nature because I interpret its perkiness as a kind of cheerful resilience.

The size of the beak and head of the sparrow is larger than you might expect. Its chest is full and the body tapers back to a no-nonsense tail. This shape gives the bird a headstrong appearance and a headlong movement: it seems to be dashing around continuously.

In summer the cock bird's head markings are neat and dapper. The 'scowl' produced by its black eye stripe flares out behind the eyes and assumes a rich chestnut brown, dividing the pale cheek patches from the crown, which is a warm slate grey.

Its back is chequered in chestnut and black – each black wing feather is edged in chestnut brown of various shades. Its summer dress is completed with a chic black bib. You can see from my studies that the bib shape twists and distorts as the bird turns its head from side to side. This is useful to remember when you are drawing and wish to convey a sense of movement.

The bird is lazy about keeping its plumage in an orderly state. It can allow the wings to fall to the side and the secondaries to flop over the primaries in recognizable masses. Sometimes it fluffs up its grey rump feathers to hide its back almost completely. The hen bird lacks the male's smart head gear, but retains the rich wing patterns.

I did a page of studies first (**fig. 86**) to reacquaint myself with the personality of the bird. Some of these studies are derived from my sketchbook and some from photographs. You will find this preliminary warm-up essential before beginning the main composition.

Fig. 86 Sketchbook studies of house sparrows

Fig. 87 *Sparrows and Clematis*

52

Fig. 88 *Starlings in Winter*

The trellis which I chose for the painting in **fig. 87** could be used as a setting for almost any garden bird – but in our garden it is the sparrows which use it most. The strong diagonals reinforce the alert pose I wanted for the birds.

The flower (simple clematis) entwined along the fence complements this unpretentious bird. When you tackle a close-up like this, take care to relate the scale of birds and flowers to each other. Here, the larger flowers emphasize the smallness of the birds.

All the detail in the flowers and birds was painted first. After masking out the flowers I washed in a purple-grey around the birds. I took care not to darken the background too much in case the result looked flat and the birds like cut-outs.

A bird artist should not approach any one species with prejudice; that way you may miss a whole world of subject matter. I say this because many people dislike another common species illustrated here – the starling; but these birds have many endearing qualities. I know they descend on the bird-table like locusts and scoff the lot. I know that their vast flocks often ruin acres of woodland. They have, however, a confident and lively nature with a touch of the comic.

Their plumage is iridescent in summer and they have pink legs and a yellow bill. In winter their plum-age is boldly spotted. The young, too, can be interesting; they don different parts of the uniform as the year progresses. Their juvenile dull tan colour may be enlivened with flank panels of polka-dotted black.

After they have fed at the bird-table, starlings will retire to a nearby tree to sit and digest quietly. All the while they will be preening, chuckling to themselves, or just contemplating. They are a picture of contentment and tranquillity. I have tried to convey some of that feeling in my painting (**fig. 88**).

I watched them for some time through binoculars and sketched, trying to grasp the birds' fundamental shapes. They carry their sharp dagger-like bills at a slight angle. The crown feathers can be raised to round up the forehead. The body is chunky and deep. They tend to raise their secondary feathers, which creates a square boxy shape. This angularity can be emphasized to suggest their rugged character.

I put down the background wash first, a pale Yellow Ochre, feeding in darker blue-grey at the top and bottom. Over this I painted the pale blue of the snow against the light. I sketched the birds in with the liner brush and then painted them in strongly with a purple-brown, criss-crossing the strokes to suggest their spotted plumage. I painted in the branches with the same colour, broken in places where the snow overlapped.

Fig. 89 Sketchbook studies of collared doves

Collared doves have colonized Britain only in the last thirty years and they make a wonderful addition to our garden birds. Their plumage is coloured in subtle hints of pastel lavenders, siennas, pinks and greys. The feathers are matt, not glossy, so the birds' form is clearly defined. This makes them a very satisfying subject to draw.

Like all doves and pigeons they are broad in the shoulders and long-necked with small heads. They are deep-bellied and the body terminates in a long rectangular tail. The bird's black necklet forms a useful punctuation mark and is helpful when you are marking out the length and breadth of the neck, whether extended or compressed.

These birds adopt marvellous poses – especially when they alight on the fence to assess the situation, craning this way and that with their long necks. They move with grace; not so fast as to be undrawable. They have a habit of raising their feathers like individual scales, clearly revealing the structural patterns of their plumage.

Fig. 89 shows a page of studies made with the liner brush. These were taken from drawings in my sketchbook; some are recent, some older. The springiness of the liner brush creates a sinuous rhythm without losing the sense of the birds' volume and weight.

I started by washing in an overall colour on the birds, a pale mix of Burnt Sienna and French Ultramarine with a tiny amount of Crimson Alizarin to warm it up. I deliberately left unpainted patches on the birds' backs and heads to suggest light falling on them. I used Burnt Umber for the primaries and a light Burnt Sienna wash for the warmer upper parts. For the necklet I used a dark version of the original overall colour. A wash of French Ultramarine was used for the shadow under the bird's body. I did not want to go into any detail for the background so I simply indicated grass or sky with a brushful of green or blue.

It is extraordinary what the addition of a wash of colour does to the drawings. It rapidly creates a feeling of space and light. The line, however, should retain the loudest voice in a study of this sort.

The tits are everyone's favourite – their liveliness, acrobatics, and vivid colouring make them a star turn. But because they are so lively and small they are one of the most difficult subjects to paint in the bird world.

If you want to, refer to photographs to begin with to familiarize yourself with the birds' markings. When

Fig. 90 Blue tits

you get down to sketching, remember, as I have told you before, that the birds will always return to a similar pose over and over again. Put down a squiggle; it is better than nothing and can always be added to later.

Look for simple shapes. The blue tit (**fig. 90**) has a roughly triangular shape with a jaunty tail stuck on behind. It has a straight back and deep chest and is almost bull-necked in appearance. It can raise its blue cap into a crest in excitement. Its eye stripe gives it a distinctly oriental expression. From the front view the pattern around its neck appears semi-circular.

The blue of the blue tit, on its head and back, is a cool one, like Cobalt Blue. It is never as bright as you think it is. The heightened colour is the result of the juxtaposition with the lemon yellow breast. Never be afraid to reduce the potency of such colours, for they will interact together to add up to more than the sum of their parts. By doing this you can also avoid that frequently encountered phenomenon, the 'kingfisher-blue blue tit'!

The great tit (**fig. 91**) derives its apparent confidence from its bold markings: contrasting black and yellow, like the wasp, recognized throughout the animal kingdom as warning colours. It has a black cap, white cheeks and a black tummy stripe. It seems to possess a mechanical precision of movement, like a clockwork toy. This impression is heightened by its repetitive call. Like the blue tit the bird is an acrobat, sometimes hanging upside down by one leg to reach a peanut.

The birds here were drawn in quickly with the liner brush and a wash of background colour was painted around and up to their outlines. I then began to put in the breast colour, Cadmium Yellow cooled with Burnt

Fig. 91 Great tits

Umber. The birds' back colour consisted of the same yellow mixed with a little French Ultramarine and Burnt Umber to tone it down to a green-grey. The 'black' of the head and the breast stripe was a mixture of Burnt Umber and French Ultramarine. In a good light the white cheeks will show up brightly, while the black head and breast absorb the light and thus create a vivid contrast of tones.

Greenfinches will come readily to nuts and seeds on the bird-table. I have counted up to twenty-seven of them in our cherry tree, waiting their turn. They are splendid finches, having a variety of greens in their plumage, with slate grey areas on their cheeks and wing feathers. Their wings and tails are also distinguished by lemon yellow patches which flash vividly when the birds take flight. The powerful bill and the legs are a contrasting pink. As spring progresses both the male and the female become greener to merge with the new foliage. Overall their general character expresses strength and solidity. They have a large squarish head and deeply notched tail.

In **fig. 92** I washed the watercolour over a pencil drawing on tinted paper. I related birds and background by using the same greens for both. Touches of light and tone pick out the birds and sunflower.

This pair visited the flower in late summer to raid the seed head. The stimulus for the picture came from the colours and from my interest in the way the sharp line of shadow from the flower cuts across the left-hand bird. The giant flower head establishes the birds' scale. The yellow petals echo the yellow bar on the birds' wings.

It is very easy to forget relative sizes in the heat of the painting process, especially if your bird is in the foreground. It is very important to make a small bird look small. Leaves and flowers can create a sense of scale if they are drawn to a comparative size.

The last composition (**fig. 93**) was inspired by my enjoyment of the flowers, Christmas roses. These grow by my sitting-room window, so I set up my easel and painted from inside. I wanted to add a bird but not one that would interfere with the shapes of the flowers; the bird was therefore secondary to the composition and had to be positioned to fit the design. I chose the blackbird as it would merge with the dark brown of the flowerbeds.

One often goes to the window and looks into the apparently deserted garden. You admire the flowers and then notice that there is a bird there after all. This is the feeling behind this painting.

Fig. 92 *Greenfinches and Sunflower*

Fig. 93 *Blackbird and Christmas Rose*

I sat down to paint the Christmas roses with their solid fingers spreading against the flagstones and the dark earth. I began by drawing in all the basic shapes with the liner brush and then underpainted using a full, pointed sable and a blue-grey wash, working out shadows and the fall of light on the leaves. Even at this stage I was not sure where I was going to put the blackbird. All the time as I worked I constantly adjusted and improved the drawing until I felt satisfied that the abstract shapes of the leaves interlocked with their background. I retained the luminosity of the flowers by working into them with the palest of tones.

The remainder of the picture descended quickly in tone. I introduced warmer tones of Burnt Umber for the soil and pebbles, and washes of pale green for the leaves. I realized now that the bird should be looking out of the picture, although positioning it so that it faced into the flowerbed could also have been interesting. Notice how its yellow eye ring and bill draw attention to its head. It was surprising, as the painting progressed, just what quantities of Burnt Umber, Burnt Sienna and other dark shades were required to capture the gloom under the leaves.

If you observe blackbirds carefully for any length of time you will realize that they are in fact anything but black. The cock bird is glossy in plumage and reflects all lights, including sky blue, in its primary and secondary feathers.

BIRDS IN THE LANDSCAPE
ASPECTS OF COMPOSITION

I have talked about colour, light and composition throughout the book. You could hardly have a painting without them! But how you use them in your picture depends primarily on what you want to say and, in the case of birds, your feelings about them and what particular aspects of their life and habitat you want to emphasize.

You may wish to describe a bird's plumage very clearly, or to suggest a particular time of day, or the weather conditions. You may perhaps want to suggest the mood you felt when you originally saw the bird. All these aims may require different approaches.

The panoramic format is very useful for organizing groups of different species. The common gull here is

Fig. 94 *Common Gull and Oystercatchers*

Fig. 95 *Resting Oystercatchers*

eyeing the oystercatchers in the hope of grabbing a free meal (**fig. 94**).

I placed the gull apart, to emphasize the togetherness of the oystercatchers. The stationary gull forms a stable counterpoint to the busily feeding birds. I subsequently modified the gull to face slightly seawards. It took me some time to realize that this would improve the picture. Together with the diagonal lines of the waves, this alteration helped to suggest space outside the composition. The ripples themselves link the separate birds. There is a full light on the birds and the background had to be reduced in overall tone to illuminate the white areas of plumage. This involved careful painting; masking fluid was useful here.

In **fig. 95** a similar group of birds is portrayed. Here, however, I wanted to express a sense of rest and tranquillity.

The quality of evening light is partly a result of the back-lit effect. This was achieved by painting light washes first and then progressively overlaying darker colours for the birds. They are almost silhouettes, compact and relaxed, although one has the feeling that the gull may have seen us and is more alert.

I grouped the central birds together to avoid monotony and left a space in front of the one on the left. The birds rise across the composition in a gentle gradient formed by the dark mud bank.

In this picture of a kingfisher (**fig. 96**), many underlying factors play their part in determining where the bird must be placed in the composition. Usually it is best to avoid placing a single bird slap in the middle of a composition. The question then is where do you put it. One practical solution to this problem is to cut out a silhouette in card of the bird you are painting and move it about over the picture surface until it finds its 'natural' place in the composition. You will find that the best position will leave a potential space for the bird to fly into. You will also find yourself avoiding the centre line of the paper, placing the bird higher up to emphasize its importance. You can then work in the bird's background around it. If you have already painted a scene and wish to place a bird, such as a kingfisher, into it you will find that the bird will form the point of interest. When considering where you want that point to be, it is important to remember size, scale and lighting.

As for colour, the kingfisher in certain lights is an electric blue, so to make it stand out it should ideally be placed on a dark background. But not uniformly dark – that would be flat and uninteresting. So why not vary

Fig. 96 *Kingfisher on the Brook*

Fig. 97 *Grey Wagtail*

Fig. 98 *Garganey and Water Lilies*

60

the background with stripes of slanting sunlight as shown here.

But what about the wagtail on the rock (**fig. 97**)? You will see that I have already changed the rules of composition here – the bird is high and to the right. I had my reasons for this; the mood I wanted to convey was the fragility of the bird, poised out of reach of the torrent. Notice I have deliberately counterbalanced the direction of the bird against the flow of the stream. This did not come about too consciously. Successful compositions are the result of thinking yourself back to or into the time and situation when you saw the bird. The painting proceeds naturally from this reliving of the experience.

If there are a number of birds in the picture then the composition is more complex. Remember that in natural habitat birds in groups still require their individual living space, otherwise quarrels break out – in itself, an interesting subject for a painting!

Placing groups of birds in the picture is not quite so difficult if they are facing in the same direction, like this group of garganey (**fig. 98**). One drake is placed further forward than the others, but all of them have a pictorial space into which they could move. The space beyond

them is suggested by the perspective of the blue water behind the lilies. Their togetherness is emphasized by their similarity of dress. Each has a white stripe over its eye which is repeated as a motif.

Even where a number of birds are facing in different directions, each bird can still have a potential space to move into. This is the case in *Partridge with Chicks* (**fig. 99**), where the birds are divided by the zigzag lines of weed and path. I have further complicated matters here by turning the birds' heads in the opposite direction from their progress. This conveys a sense of concern for the safety of the chicks. The viewer tends, like them, to look both ways as well.

The birds are back-lit, so their plumage shares illuminated edges with the leaves, flowers and stones. The vegetation half conceals the birds, which suggests how secretive they are at this time of year.

The format of the painting in **fig. 100** was determined by the requirements for a magazine cover. Such restrictions can be very stimulating. This tall, narrow shape immediately projects an active and energetic feeling and has other advantages in that, like the panoramic format, it makes it easy to concentrate attention on any part of the picture area.

Fig. 99 *Partridge with Chicks*

61

Fig. 100 *Little Gulls in Spring*

In this painting I tried to recall a sense of looking upwards at the birds. I was sitting on the ground as I watched them. The lower birds were almost at eye level, and as they mounted higher they presented more underwing. I wanted to convey the 'whirling leaves' impression that this flock of small gulls gave me. They would intermittently 'dance' off to disappear high over the lake, then reappear like a bunch of controlled snowflakes to perch and preen on these lakeside posts.

The flying birds moving off in various flight patterns suggest a sense of free-falling, while the perched birds provide a fixed visual point, a centre of gravity in all this cascading movement.

The permutations of direction and position of the birds which are possible in a composition of this sort are limitless. I tried dozens of variations; after much drawing and retracing and many paintings, I decided that this one was the most successful.

The birds themselves show juvenile and adult plumage in various states of completion. An added complication in portraying them was the fact that these birds have a charcoal black underwing, which in visual terms suggests heaviness. This could have counteracted the birds' delightful grace and lightness. It is helpful here to remember the amount of reflected light from the surface of the ground or water there is on the underwing of a bird in flight, even if it is unusually dark like the little gull's wing. If you then consider the amount of light streaming across the field of view and softening the birds' colours, and the similar effect that distance gives, you can see that there is plenty of opportunity to overcome visual problems of this kind.

The principle of allowing birds space in which to move applies to flying birds, too (**fig. 101**). When the birds are in the distance a sense of anticipation is created. But in this picture of wild swans they have already passed across the centre of vision and there is a farewell mood to the picture, enhanced by the blue-grey tones of the landscape and sky. The sweep of the clouds enlarges the space and appears to help the birds on their journey. The ditch below turns to the left in a counterpoint, linking us, the observers, with the distant low horizon. The hawthorn tree provides a central point around which everything else moves. As for the birds, my arrangement of lowering the leading pair suggests their struggle as they climb for height.

When composing large flocks or skeins of birds in the sky it helps to imagine a thread joining them; and this line itself can suggest the rhythm of flight.

A different matter, however, is close-up flight, such as shown in **fig. 102**, which illustrates a marsh harrier closing on a young coot. They, too, are connected by an imaginary cord. The small dark bird counterpoints the larger but lighter bird of prey, which half turns towards us and the coot. This movement is echoed in the landscape and the clouds. Note that the 'horizon' line is well above the middle of the picture, which has the effect of placing the observer down among the reeds.

I hope these guidelines have given you some help with your composition. There is plenty of scope for fresh ideas. The best compositions derive from your strength of feeling about the birds you see – first impressions put down quickly are often the best. Always work up from small sketches first. Plenty of preparation means that the painting, when it begins, will flow more easily and successfully.

Fig. 101 *Wild Swans*

Fig. 102 *Marsh Harrier Surprising a Young Coot, Norfolk*

A FEW LAST WORDS

Fig. 103 *Willow Warbler and May Blossom*

I hope the ideas in this book have helped you if you paint already. If you do not, I hope it has encouraged you to take a look at the bird world for inspiration. It's a world of breathtaking beauty, and paper and paint seem very inadequate sometimes to convey this. If your progress seems to creep at a snail's pace and frustration sets in, don't despair. The answer is to go out and look at the birds again. Refresh yourself from the source and inspiration will return.

I like to think of the bird artist as the invisible observer, witnessing and passing without trace while the birds live their lives oblivious of his or her presence. Many bird paintings express this feeling, in fact.

It is a delightful fantasy, of course, the idea of floating invisibly about the countryside; but it is something to aspire to, even if it's only to practise some fieldcraft. It is always very satisfactory to leave the birds, animals and the countryside as undisturbed as possible both at your arrival on the scene and at your departure.

I am very cautious about drawing birds on or near their nests. In fact, the same laws about this apply to artists as to photographers. These are laid down by the Nature Conservancy Council. Permission must be obtained from them when photographing and therefore when drawing or painting uncommon or endangered species on the nest.

All birds, bar a small handful of species, are of course now protected. Make sure you obtain from the Royal Society for the Protection of Birds a copy of the list of protected species, and the rules laid down by the Society for studying birds without disturbing them. These rules, distilled from a hundred years of experience, set out in detail what you may or may not do. Happy painting!